Serif
Inspiring Creativity

PagePlus. X9
Quick Start Guide

Simple steps for creating
great-looking publications.

Visual reference

 In this guide, we will refer to specific tools, toolbars, tabs, or menus. Use this visual reference to help locate them on the PagePlus workspace.

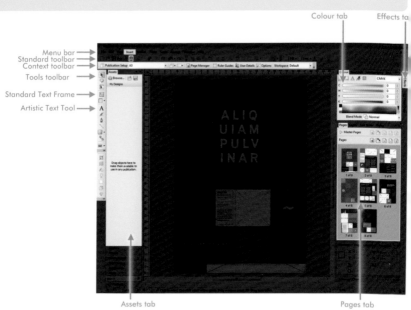

Menu bar
Standard toolbar
Context toolbar
Tools toolbar
Standard Text Frame
Artistic Text Tool

Colour tab
Effects tab

Assets tab

Pages tab

This Quick Start Guide will walk you through the key stages in getting started with PagePlus, creating a brochure and business card along the way, and explain how to publish your project.

Installation

To install PagePlus X9, insert the PagePlus X9 program disc into your disc drive. The AutoRun feature automatically starts the setup process. Simply answer the on-screen questions to install.

Contents

Starting PagePlus

When you launch PagePlus, the **Startup Assistant** appears.

The assistant lets you create new publications from templates or from scratch, open PagePlus publications, and access articles (tutorials, news, and more) from Serif's Learn and News feeds.

For this Quick Start Guide, we'll create a brochure from a Theme Layout template and a simple business card from scratch using the **Templates** and **New Publication** buttons.

You don't need to start from scratch with PagePlus. Instead, you can create a complete publication based entirely on a theme layout (i.e., a set of pre-designed template pages with a similar look and feel).

To pick your design, simply select a theme layout and a colour scheme to suit your taste.

From a template

1. On the left of the **Startup Assistant**, click **Templates**.

   The Templates pane appears.

2. From the left, select the type of publication (e.g., Brochures) and then from the right, a theme for that publication (e.g., Partition).

3. (Optional) Next, select a colour scheme.

4. (Optional) Uncheck any pages you don't want in your publication.

5. Click **OK**.

Adding user details

When you create a publication from a design template, you may be prompted to update your user details (Name, Company, Address, etc). PagePlus will use these details to personalize your publication and then store them for you to use in future publications.

1. In the displayed **User Details** dialog, enter your user details. This information will be used to populate the contact details on the front and back pages.

2. Click **Update**.

* Names and addresses are fictitious; for example use only.

For our brochure, we can add extra blank or unused template pages to build up our publication.

Viewing pages

1. At the right of your workspace, click the **Pages** tab.

2. Double-click a page to display it in your workspace.

Adding pages

1. In the **Pages** tab, select a page (e.g., page 3 of 8) by clicking once on its thumbnail.

2. Click 🗋 **Add** to add a page before the selected page.

Deleting pages

• Select a page (e.g., page 8) in the **Pages** tab, and then click 🗋 **Delete**. In the dialog, click **Yes**.

Assigning master pages

Master pages are great for applying the same underlying page design across your publication.

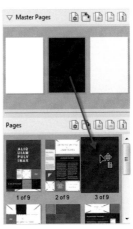

1. On the **Pages** tab, click **Master Pages**.

2. Drag a master page from the window onto a page (e.g., page 3) in the lower **Pages** window.

In PagePlus, there are a range of assets that you can use to personalize your publications. These range from graphics and backgrounds, to page content and layouts.

Adding page content

1. On the **Assets** tab to the left of your workspace, choose the **Page Content** category.

2. Display page 3 from the Pages tab by double-clicking.

3. From the **Assets** tab, drag your chosen content onto the page and then position it as required.

Graphics
Pictures
Picture Frames
Page Content
Backgrounds
Pages
Search

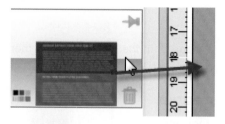

 Select another category from the left to browse the other types of assets available.

 You can also click **Browse** at the top of the **Assets** tab to add additional assets from any asset pack.

Edit the brochure heading

1. On the **Pages** tab, double-click the first page to display it in your workspace.

2. Hold Ctrl and click-drag a corner handle to resize the main heading box, making it wider.

1 of 8

3. Triple-click on the main heading and type your text.

Edit body text

1. On page 2, triple-click on a text frame to select a paragraph. You can replace this placeholder text with your own text.

2. Type your text.

 For more editing options, click to set an insertion point to begin typing or double-click a word and type to replace it.

Pictures

Add your own pictures to your publication via the **Assets** tab.

Adding pictures

1. On the **Assets** tab, select the **Pictures** category.

2. Click **Add** at the bottom of the category.

3. Navigate to, then select your pictures (try **Ctrl**-click to select multiple pictures), and click **Open**. The pictures are added to the tab category.

4. Drag your chosen picture onto a page (e.g., page 3).

5. Resize and/or rotate your picture using the corner or rotate handles, respectively.

Adding effects to pictures

You can add stylish effects to your pictures from the **Effects** tab.

1. With your picture selected, click the **Effects** tab to expand (top right of your workspace).

2. Click ☐ next to an effect in the list (e.g., Drop Shadow) to enable it.

3. Adjust the effect by moving the sliders.

Adding pictures to picture frames

Your brochure is based on a themed layout, so empty placeholder picture frames can be filled with your pictures.

1. Display page 1 from the **Pages** tab by double-clicking.

2. Drag from the **Assets** tab's **Pictures** category onto an empty picture frame.

Cutting out

1. Above your selected picture, on the context toolbar, click ✎ **Cutout Studio.**

2. In the studio, use the circular cursor to paint over areas to discard.

3. At the bottom right of **Cutout Studio**, click ◉ **Preview** to review your cutout, and click ✓ OK.

Use the ✎ **Keep brush** to paint over areas to keep if you've accidentally discarded too much.

Starting from scratch

You can also create new publications from scratch which gives you more design freedom.

Starting a new publication

1. On the left of the **Startup Assistant,** click **New Publication.**

    The **Page Setup** pane appears.

2. Scroll down the pane and select a publication type (e.g., Small Publications - Business Cards) and a page orientation that you want to start with (e.g., Wide Business Cards).

The blank page is displayed in the workspace.

 You can access the Startup Assistant any time using the **File** menu.

Inserting User Details

No business card would be complete without contact details. If you entered your user details when creating the brochure, you can insert these now. This saves you typing them twice and allows you to add your full contact details to any publication.

1. From the **Tools** toolbar, click 🖺 **Standard Text Frame.**

2. Drag a text box out on your page.

3. From the context toolbar above your page, set your preferred font and font size for your text, e.g.

4. From the **Insert** menu, select **Information** > **User Details**.

5. Select an entry marked '(Business)' from the list and click **OK**.

6. Repeat this process to add the remaining user details.

You'll end up with a continuous list of user details that can now be formatted.

 If you haven't entered your user details yet, you can do this by clicking  **User Details** on the Page context toolbar.

Formatting text

Let's format the user details list to be more presentable.

1. After each user detail entry, click to display a flashing insertion point, and press **Shift-Return** to insert soft returns.

2. Click and drag across the company name to select.

3. From the context toolbar, select a font size of '12 pt'.

4. From the **Colour** tab, choose a colour (e.g., RGB 232:152:39).

Magnus Tyrell
Deckard Industries
233 Harris Avenue
Loros Langdon
E17 2BC

www.deckardindustries.com
magnus@deckardindustries.com

Adding a picture

1. Select **Import Picture** from the **Tools** toolbar on the left, navigate and select your picture, then click **Open**.

2. To set the picture size, drag the cursor across your page and release the mouse button.

3. Rotate your picture by dragging the ⚓ rotate handle at the top of the picture.

4. To finish off, add an Inner Shadow effect (**Effects** tab; top-right, presented vertically) to make your framed picture really stand out!

Magnus Tyrell
Deckard Industries
233 Harris Avenue
Loros Langdon
E17 2BC

www.deckardindustries.com
magnus@deckardindustries.com

To add a background or other assets to your publication, simply choose a category from the left of the Asset Browser.

Contents

D1363745

Contents

Welcome

Welcome!

Welcome to **PagePlus X9**, the award-winning Desktop Publishing (DTP) solution from Serif that lets you create, publish and share designs as outstanding printed documents, stunning PDFs, PDF slideshows, tables/charts, modern eBooks or via web page.

PagePlus comes with an impressive selection of **design templates**, **creative content**, and styles for you to use. As a result, publishing to a professional standard is easily achievable for experienced and inexperienced users alike! You'll also be able to reuse existing content by importing PDF documents and word processing documents.

Upgrading?

If you've upgraded from a previous version, this new edition of PagePlus includes a host of **exciting** new features which keeps PagePlus ahead of its competitors and at a fraction of the price! We hope you also enjoy the additional power and performance edge.

Registration

Don't forget to register your new copy, using the **Registration Wizard**, on the **Help** menu. That way, we can keep you informed of new developments and future upgrades!

New features

New features are fully described in PagePlus Help, with many also being covered in tutorials in the Startup Assistant's Learn feed.

Here's a summary of PagePlus X9's new features..

- **PDF Publishing enhancements**
  Now compatible with PDF/X-4 and PDF/X-5, which support transparency, PagePlus keeps up to date with the latest PDF standards.

- **Placed PDF pass-through**
  Any placed PDF in your publication is honoured with absolute fidelity using pass-through.

- **Auto-flowing text frames**
  Automatically create, or remove, text frames as text content is added to, or deleted from, the publication page. This makes PagePlus similar to a word processor's approach to frame control.

- **QR codes**
  QR codes make online information accessible to handheld scanners or smart phones. Simply scan the code in a printed or electronic publication to view **text** or **web addresses**; make contact by **email**, **telephone** or **SMS message**; even add **VCards** or **VEvents** to your device's contacts or calendar. QR code fields can be included in **mail merge operations** too!

- **More powerful Calendar Event Manager**
  In a newly designed month-to-view event calendar, events are now stored in iCalendar files, and can be categorized into **event types**, e.g., business, personal, world. Each category can be switched on or off per publication and are colour coded for easier event identification. Any iCalendar file can be **imported**; you can **export** your calendar events too!

Ease of Use

- **Easier ruler guide control**
  For precision placement, use the **Transform tab** to position guides. For quicker guide setup, the **Guide Tool** offers **selectable** guides which lets you move, duplicate, copy/paste (to another page), distribute or delete multiple guides simultaneously. Ruler guides can now be viewed independently of margin, row/column and bleed area guides.

- **Tool feedback**
  As a useful design aid, object resizing and rotating, shape modifying and table row/column insertion now report values on the object as they change.

- **Master page improvements**
  For easier identification, master pages can be **named**. As a time saver, swap out or add additional master pages to **multiple pages** in one operation.

Import and Export

- **WebP import and export**
  This relatively new graphics format is designed for web use as it produces lower file sizes compared to PNG while still supporting lossless transparency.

- **Add DrawPlus designs without graphics export**
  Place DrawPlus X8 designs, as their original project files, on your PagePlus page. Either embed or link (to update design changes without reimport).

- **EPS export**
  Supports export to EPS files including settings for compatibility, colour properties and overprinting.

Text

- **Copy text properties with Format Painter**
  As well as copying an object's formatting, any selected text's formatting can now be applied to other artistic and frame text.

- **Convert frame text to table**
  PagePlus can detect different text deliminators (commas, tab marks, and more) in text frames and convert selected delimited text to tables with no fuss.

Checking your Work

- **Better cross-language spelling check and hyphenation**
  Install open source **Hunspell** dictionaries, as used in OpenOffice® and LibreOffice® programs, for versatile spell checking and hyphenation of text across many languages.

Pro Typography

- **Kerning control**
  Improved kerning that adopts the latest GPOS kerning control.

- **Spacing options for more flexible pagination**
  Suppress spacing between paragraphs of same style, remove suppression of 'Space before' at start of text frame/column, and combine 'Space after' and 'Space before' between adjacent paragraphs.

Installation

Installing PagePlus follows different procedures depending on whether
you are installing from disc or via download.

> You can install your new version alongside previous versions and use
> them independently.
>
> 32 or 64-bit PagePlus X9 installs to respective 32 or 64-bit computers.

Installation procedure (from disc)

- Insert your purchased disc into your disc drive.

    - If AutoPlay is enabled on the drive, this automatically starts the
      Setup Wizard. Follow the on-screen instructions for install.

      -or-

    - If AutoPlay is not enabled (or doesn't start the install
      automatically), navigate to your program disc and double-click
      autorun.exe.

Installation procedure (from download)

- From **serif.com**, when logged into your Serif account, follow the
  on-screen instructions to download.

System Requirements

Minimum:

- Windows-based PC* with mouse or equivalent input device

- Operating systems:
  Windows® 10, 8, 7, Vista (32 or 64 bit)
  Microsoft Windows® XP SP3 (32 bit)

- 512MB RAM (Windows® XP)
  1GB RAM (Windows® Vista and 32-bit Windows 7® and 8)
  2GB RAM (For 64-bit Windows® 7, 8, 10)

- 564MB free hard disk space for physical media install
  (and a DVD drive)
  1.66GB free hard disk space for download install (additional space
  required during installation)

- 1024 x 768 monitor resolution (at 100% scaling)

* Main processor must support SSE2 instructions.

Additional disk resources and memory are required when editing large
and/or complex publications.

Recommended

As above but:

- Dual-core processor technology

Optional:

- Windows-compatible printer

- TWAIN-compatible scanner and/or digital camera

- .NET 2.0 for text import filters (Word 2007/2010 + OpenOffice) (installed by default)*

- Internet account and connection required for accessing online resources

* On Windows 8/10, also requires an extra 1GB of free hard disk space.

Getting Started

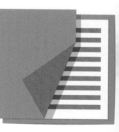

2

Startup Assistant

Once PagePlus has been installed, you're ready to start.

- For Windows Vista/7/10: Use the Windows **Start** button to pop up the Start menu, click on **All Programs (All apps)** and then click **Serif PagePlus X9**.

- For Windows 8: Use the Windows **Start** button to pop up the startup screen, and then click the PagePlus icon.

On program launch, the Startup Assistant is displayed which offers different routes into PagePlus:

The options are described as follows:

-  The default home page keeps you in touch with Serif promotions and showcases articles (tutorials, etc.) You can also view the PagePlus Overview and Quick Start video

- **Open** - to access PagePlus publications, PDF files, or BookPlus files; also provides recent file history.

- **Learn** - for online video/written tutorials, help, tips & tricks, and more—all via a learn feed that can be filtered by article Type. The Product Help and your PagePlus X9 user guide are also provided.

- **New Publication** - creates a new publication from scratch, based on a choice of page setups.

- **Templates** - creates a new publication based on one of many design templates.

- **News** - for cross-product news, company news, articles, and product announcements, using Serif's news feed.

Any time you access the Startup Assistant, the Learn or News buttons indicate the number of new articles to be viewed (if available). This number will decrease as you read each article in the Learn or News pane.

When new articles arrive, these will be indicated the next time you open the Startup Assistant.

Any new unread article arriving in the Learn or News pane will display a "new" indicator in its thumbnail.

Once you've clicked on a new article the "new" indicator changes to a "read" indicator.

Don't forget to use the keyword Search box at the top-right of the Startup Assistant. This is an incredibly powerful tool for filtering specific publication names, Learn articles, page sizes, theme layout names, or news articles.

Creating a publication from a design template

PagePlus comes complete with a whole range of categorized design templates which will speed you through the creation of all kinds of publications for desktop or commercial printing!

Each template offers:

- **Complementary design**—Professionally designed layout with high-visual impact.

- **Schemes**—choose a named colour scheme to apply a specific look and feel.

Design templates come in two types—**Theme Layouts**, where you pick your own pictures, or ready-to-go **Pro Templates** which are already populated with pictures.

Theme layouts offer a choice of themes (e.g., Ribbon) on which to base your publication (Brochure, Business Card, Flyer, Forms, Letterheads, Newsletter, ePublication, etc.); you'll get picture placeholders instead of actual pictures. Simply add your own pictures to placeholders and personalize placeholder text, then publish.

You can also choose which page layouts you want to base your new publication on.

Ready-to-go Pro templates

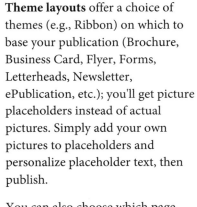

These are categorized templates containing royalty-free photos which can be adopted to fast-track you to your completed publication. You just need to personalize placeholder text, then publish.

To create a publication from a design template:

1. Open PagePlus, or select **Startup Assistant** from the **File** menu.

2. Click **Templates**.

3. From the pane, select a Theme Layout or a design template from the Pro Template Packs category. Select from the tree menu in the left-hand pane. Alternatively, scroll down to choose a publication type from the same list, e.g. Brochures, Business Cards, ePublications, etc.

4. Navigate the main window's categories and sub-categories using the ⊙ and ⊙ buttons to expand and collapse, then click your chosen thumbnail.

5. Examine the page sample(s) on the right. For theme layouts with multiple pages (e.g., brochures), you can choose which pages you wish to be part of your publication by checking the check box under each page. For design templates, simply review the pages to be part of your publication.

Theme Layouts   *Pro Design Templates*

6. Pick a **colour scheme** from the drop-down list at the top of the dialog. The page thumbnails refresh to reflect the new page's appearance.

7. Click **OK**. The pages are added to your new publication.

Starting a new publication from scratch

Although **design templates** can simplify your design choices, you can just as easily start out from scratch with a new, blank publication.

Page sizes are available for a range of publications including business cards, labels, and posters, with support for folded and ePublication publication setup.

To start a new publication (via Startup Assistant):

1. Open PagePlus to display the **Startup Assistant**.
   - or -
   Select **Startup Assistant** from the **File** menu (during your session).

2. Select **New Publication**.

3. From the main pane, navigate the document categories by scrolling (click the ⊙ icon to collapse categories if needed).

4. Click a thumbnail to create your new blank publication.

To create a publication using the default page type:

- During your PagePlus session, click 🗋 **New Publication** on the **Standard** toolbar.

To create a custom publication:

1. From the Startup Assistant's New Publication pane, click **Custom Publication**.

2. From the Publication Setup dialog, select a publication type, size, and orientation.

3. Click **OK**.

> Choosing an **Intent** from **File>Publication Setup** which will help PagePlus more accurately represent how your publication will look when published or printed. Choose between the two **Print/PDF** and **eBook/Web** output types, preferably before you start creating content. You can also choose a colour mode (RGB or CMYK) that suits either on-screen viewing or printed output, respectively.

Opening existing publications

You can open a PagePlus publication from the **Startup Assistant**, **Standard** toolbar, or via the **File** menu.

It is also possible to open PDF files as new publications, or Import PDF files and existing PagePlus files into currently open publications. (See PagePlus Help for these import options.)

To open an existing publication (via Startup Assistant):

1. Open PagePlus to display the initial **Startup Assistant**.
    - or -
    Select **Startup Assistant** from the **File** menu (during your session).

2. Select **Open**.

3. Several options are possible:

    i.   For recently opened publications, select a thumbnail from the main pane.

    ii. The publication opens in your workspace.

        - or -

i. For other PagePlus publications, PDF files, or BookPlus files, select from the Browse My Computer pane.

ii. From the dialog, locate and select your file, then click **Open**.

To open existing publications (without Startup Assistant):

• Click **Open** on the **Standard** toolbar.

Object management overview

Action	Tool/button/ command name	Toolbar/ Tab/key
Aligning	Align Objects	**Arrange** toolbar
	Align Top	**Align** tab
	Align Bottom	
	Align Left	
	Align Right	
	Horizontal Centre	
	Vertical Centre	
Combining	Convert to>Curves then Combine Curves	**Tools** menu then **Arrange** menu
Copying	Copy	**Standard** toolbar
Cropping	Square Crop Tool	**Attributes** toolbar

Cutting	✂ Cut	**Standard** toolbar
Delete		**Delete** Key
Distributing	Space Evenly Across Space Evenly Down	**Align** tab
Duplicating	-	-
Flip (horizontally)	Flip horizontal	**Arrange** menu
Flipping (vertically)	Flip vertical	**Arrange** menu
Grouping	Group/ Ungroup	Under selected objects
Joining	Join Outlines	**Arrange** toolbar
Locking/ Unlocking	-	**Arrange** menu>Lock Object **Arrange** menu>Unlock Objects
Moving	Pointer Tool	**Tools** toolbar
Ordering	Bring to Front Send to Back Forward One Back One	**Arrange** toolbar

Pasting	Paste	**Standard** toolbar
Placing	Place Multiple	**Context** toolbar
Selecting	Pointer Tool / Lasso Tool	**Tools** toolbar
Replicating	-	**Edit** menu
Resizing	Pointer Tool	**Tools** toolbar
Rotating	Pointer Tool	**Tools** toolbar
	Rotate Left / Rotate Right	**Arrange** toolbar

Saving your publication

To save your work:

1. Click ▦ **Save** on the **Standard** toolbar.

2. To save under a different name, choose **Save As** from the **File** menu.

> Unsaved publications have an asterisk after their name in the PagePlus title bar, **Publications** toolbar, and **Window** menu.

Updating and saving defaults

Object defaults are the stored property settings PagePlus applies to newly created objects such as:

- **lines** and **shapes** (line and fill colour, shade, pattern, transparency, etc.)

- **frames** (margins, columns, etc.)

- **text** (i.e., font, size, colour, alignment, etc.). Defaults are saved separately for **artistic, shape**, **frame** and **table text.**

You can easily change the defaults for any type of object via the **Update Object Default** command or the **Text Style Palette** dialog.

Default settings are always **local**—that is, any changed defaults apply to the current publication and are automatically saved with it, so they're in effect next time you open that publication. However, at any time you can use the **Save Defaults** command to record the current defaults as **global** settings that will be in effect for any new publication you subsequently create.

To set local defaults for a particular type of object:

1. Create a single sample object and fine-tune its properties as desired—or use an existing object with the right properties.

2. Select the object that's the basis for the new defaults and from the **Format** menu, select **Update Object Default** .

Or, for line and fill colours, including line styles:

1. With no object selected, choose the required line and/or fill colours from the Colour or Swatches tab. Use the Line tab to set a default line weight, style, and corner shape.

2. Draw your object on the page, which will automatically adopt the newly defined default colours and styles.

To view and change default text properties:

1. From the **Format** menu, select **Text Style Palette**.

2. Double-click **Default Text**, then from the expanded list of text types, choose an option (e.g., Artistic Text).

3. Click **Modify** to view current settings for the selected text type.

4. Use the dialog to alter character, paragraph, or other properties.

To save all current defaults as global settings:

1. From the **Tools** menu, select **Save Default Settings**.

2. From the dialog, check options to update specific defaults globally:

    *   **Document and object defaults** - saves current settings.

    *   **Text styles** - saves current text styles in the Text Style Palette.

    *   **Object styles** - saves user-defined styles from Styles tab.

3. Click **Save** to confirm that you want new publications to use the checked object's defaults globally.

Pages

3

Setting up a publication

A publication's **page size**, **orientation** and **intent** settings are fundamental to your layout, and are defined when the new publication is first created, either **using a design template** or as a **new publication**.

To adjust size/orientation of the current publication:

1. Select ▣ **Publication Setup** from the Pages context toolbar.

2. Ensure the **Paper** menu option is selected. The other option, **Margins**, lets you define non-printable Margin, Row, Column, and Bleed Guides as design aids.

3. For a **Regular/Booklet Publication**, you can select a pre-defined paper size, printer-derived paper size, or enter custom values for page **Width** and **Height**, as well as setting the orientation (Portrait or Landscape). For booklets only, select a type from the **Booklet** drop-down list, which page to start on (left/right), and if you require **Facing pages** (including **Dual master pages**). PagePlus automatically performs **imposition**.

4. For other publication types, you can select: **Small Publications** (for example, business cards, labels, etc.), **Large Publications** (banners or posters), or **Folded Publications** (cards).

    -   For Small publications, enable **Paper** and choose a pre-defined option from the list, or for creating **Labels**, enable the radio button and pick an Avery label code which matches your labels.

    -   For Large and Folded publications, choose a pre-defined option from the list (use the preview).

5. Click **OK** to accept the new dimensions. The updated settings will be applied to the current publication.

⚠ Be sure to set an appropriate **Intent** for your publication.

Once you've set up your publication, you can optionally include repeated page elements on every page by creating **master pages** (p. 29).

Intent

Setting the intent for your publication determines how text is composed and rendered, so should be decided at the start of your project.

> ⚠ Changing intent after you've finished designing can alter the appearance of your publication and can affect text flow. You may need to adjust text frame sizes and layouts.

1. In the **Publication Setup** dialog, click the **Intent** menu option.

2. Set the **Destination** to 'Print / PDF' or 'eBook / Web'.

   PagePlus composes text for Print/PDF output by default, so you should change it if publishing digitally as an eBook/web page, or designing for dual-purpose print and digital publishing.

3. Set the **Primary Colour Mode** to **RGB** or **CMYK**.

   This controls whether the publication uses a colour system that is most suitable for viewing on-screen (**RGB**) or for printing (**CMYK**) based on professional print inks.

> 🖸 If a preflight warning indicates an incorrect document intent, the offered 'fix' will automatically change the intent in this dialog to match the output to be published to.

> 💡 If producing work professionally you may want to enable colour management. The publication's primary colour mode is also set in the **Colour Management** dialog.

Uniform and mixed page orientations

If you've changed your mind about the page orientation chosen at page setup, you can change the page orientation uniformly across your publication at any time.

1 of 4

2 of 4

3 of 4

4 of 4

To change all publication pages from portrait to landscape (or vice versa):

- On the Pages context toolbar, click the down arrow on the **Publication Orientation** button, then select **Landscape Publication** (or **Portrait Publication**) from the flyout.

To change a page from portrait to landscape (or vice versa):

1. On the Pages tab, double-click to select a page.

2. Click **Change page orientation** to swap between portrait and landscape orientation.

- or -

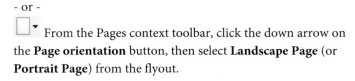 From the Pages context toolbar, click the down arrow on the **Page orientation** button, then select **Landscape Page** (or **Portrait Page**) from the flyout.

You can repeat the procedure for any other selected page.

Adding, removing, and rearranging pages

Use the **Pages tab** to add/delete standard or **master pages**, **assign master pages** to standard pages, and rearrange standard pages using drag-and-drop. You can also change **page orientations**.

To add a single page:

1. On the **Pages** tab, click once to select a page in the **Pages** window. The thumbnail that's shown as "selected" is independent of the page you're currently working on. To work on a particular page, double-click its thumbnail.

2. Click **Add** to add a page (or master page) *before* the one selected in the window.
    - or -
    To add a new page *at the end* of the publication, deselect all pages by clicking in the neutral region of the lower window, then click the **Add** button.

To add master pages:

For **master pages**, the above procedure applies but you need to click **Master Pages** to open its window first.

To delete a single page/master page:

1. On the **Pages** tab, select the page (or master page) to delete on the appropriate window by clicking its thumbnail.

2. Click **Delete Page/Remove Master Page**.

To rearrange pages:

*   On the **Pages** tab, in the lower **Pages** window, drag a page thumbnail over another page thumbnail in the page sequence. The page is added after the hovered over page thumbnail.

Adding more template pages

Use the Assets tab's Asset Browser if you're looking to use some additional template pages in your publication. See **Browsing** on p. 41.

You can drag-and-drop a page to replace (or add before/after) your current page.

> Currently used pages can be stored for future use by clicking **Add** on the Assets tab's Pages category. See Storing designs in PagePlus Help.

Understanding master pages

Master pages provide a flexible way to store background elements that you'd like to appear on more than one page—for example a logo, background, header/footer, or border design.

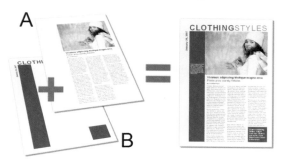

(**A**) Page, (**B**) Master Page

The key concept here is that a particular master page is typically **shared** by multiple pages, as illustrated below. By placing a design element on a master page and then assigning several pages to use that master page, you ensure that all the pages incorporate that element. Of course, each individual page can have its own "foreground" elements.

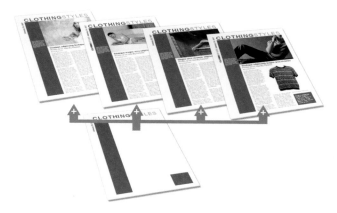

Master pages are available in every publication, but in a simple publication you may not need to use any master pages—or you may need only one master page. Facing pages and multiple master pages prove valuable with longer, more complex publications.

 If you're starting with a design template you may encounter one or more master pages incorporated with the design.

Using the **Pages** tab or **Master Page Manager**, you can quickly add or delete master pages; for example, you could set up different master pages for "title" or "chapter divider" pages.

Assigning master pages

If you're only using one master page it is assigned to any newly created page by default. However, if you have multiple master pages you can swap a page's master page for another or add additional master pages to a page. This is not restricted to an individual page as you can also work on selected, odd, even or all pages.

 You'll need to create an additional master page first. See **Adding, removing, and rearranging pages** on p. 27.

To swap one page's master page for another:

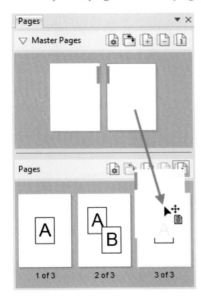

- From the expanded Master Pages window in the Pages tab, drag a master page onto a target standard page in the lower window.

> Click **Page Identifiers** to indicate the master pages used on the currently selected page(s). The master page is represented as a letter on the Page, e.g. A, B, C, etc.

To swap multiple page's master page for another:

1. In the Pages tab, select pages in the lower window using **Shift**-click or **Ctrl**-click for adjacent or non-adjacent pages, respectively.

2. Right-click any selected page, and choose **Remove Master Pages**.

3. Right-click any selected page again, and choose **Add Master Page**.

4. Select the replacement master page from the dialog.

5. Click **OK**.

Assigning multiple master pages

You can assign additional master pages to your page for more powerful page design.

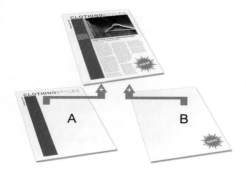

In the example above, both master page 'A' and master page 'B' contribute to the page design (shown at top).

 An additional master page needs to be created first. See **Adding, removing, and rearranging pages** on p. 27.

To add an additional master page to an individual page:

- On the **Pages** tab, **Ctrl**-drag a master page thumbnail from the Master Page window onto the chosen page's thumbnail in the Pages window. The chosen page must have a master page assigned already.

To add an additional master page to selected pages:

1. In the Pages tab, select pages in the lower window using **Shift**-click or **Ctrl**-click for adjacent or non-adjacent pages, respectively.

2. Right-click any selected page again, and choose **Add Master Page**.

3. Select the additional master page from the dialog.

4. Click **OK**.

Facing pages and dual master pages

If you're using multi-page **regular/booklet publications**, you can assign different master pages to the left and right publication pages (also called spreads) if necessary—master pages are assigned per page and not per spread. For example (see below), a left-hand "body text" page might use the left-side component of one master page (**A**), while a right-hand page could use the right side of a different master page (**B**).

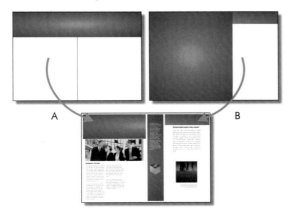

Editing master page objects

If you're editing pages which use master pages, master page objects will contribute to your page design. These objects can be edited quickly and easily from the page by using a control bar under the selected object.

- Click ➕A **Edit on Master Page** to jump to the master page and edit the object there.

- Click ⌃A **Promote from Master Page** to disconnect the object from the master page and make it independently editable on the publication page.

Using page numbering

Page number fields automatically display the current page number. Typically, these fields are added automatically to the **master page** (so they appear on every page) with the Header and Footers Wizard (**Insert** menu), but you can insert a page number field anywhere in your master page text.

You can change the style of page numbers, create mixed page number formats, set starting page number(s), and control number continuation across chapters and publication sections (all via **Page Number Format** on the **Format** menu).

To insert a page number field:

1. Switch to the master page (if desired) by clicking A1 **View Master Pages** on the Hintline.

2. With the **Artistic Text Tool** selected (**Tools** toolbar), click for an insertion point to place the page number.

3. On the **Insert** menu, select **Page Number** from the **Information** flyout.

You can also specify the **First Page Number** in the sequence (this will appear on the first page of the publication). For example, Chapter Two of a long publication might be in a separate file and begin numbering with page 33.

To set the first page number:

1. Uncheck **Continue from previous chapter**. PagePlus keeps this checked by default so that number continuation is maintained if your publication is to be part of a book.

2. Enter a different **First Page Number**.

For more complex publications, different formats can be used for different page ranges. See PagePlus Help.

Navigating pages

To switch between pages:

*   On the **Pages** tab, double-click the page's thumbnail for the page (or master page) you want to view.

To switch between current page and its master page:

*   From the **Hintline**, click **Master Pages**.

Assets for Creativity

4

Using assets

An **asset** is a general term for any object or page element that can be added to your page to enhance its appearance, increase efficiency, or personalize your design. Assets range from graphics, logos, **pictures**, picture **frames**, and backgrounds (as shown below), to more complex page content and entire pages.

To use assets, PagePlus provides the **Assets tab**, powered by both an **Asset Browser** (p. 41) and Asset Manager. The former browses your assets, the latter lets you create and manage custom Asset Packs.

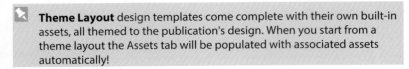

Theme Layout design templates come complete with their own built-in assets, all themed to the publication's design. When you start from a theme layout the Assets tab will be populated with associated assets automatically!

Using the Assets tab

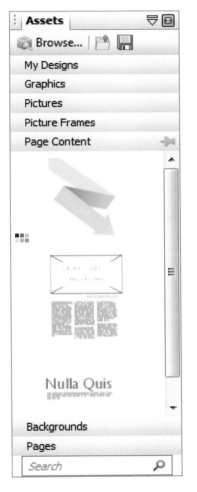

The Assets tab is a powerful design resource that exclusively hosts your browsed assets, ready for adding to your publication page.

Assets can be placed into the following categories.

- **My Designs**: Stores custom assets dragged from the page.

- **Graphics**: Stores professional clipart from Asset Packs.

- **Pictures**: Stores added pictures from your hard disk (or from Asset Pack, if containing pictures).

- **Picture Frames**: Stores picture frames from Asset Packs.

- **Page Content**: Stores page content (pre-assembled from various page objects) from Asset Packs.

- **Backgrounds**: Stores backgrounds from Asset Packs.

- **Pages**: Stores complete ready-to-go pages from Asset Packs.

The tab also lets you create custom designs for reuse globally or just in your publication. You'll be able to:

- Store your own designs to the tab's My Designs category for global use.

- Store your own designs to any other tab's category for current publication use.

- Create custom **picture frames** from drawn shapes.

- Create custom page backgrounds from pictures or filled page objects.

- Create custom page content (combinations of assets).

Although initially empty, the tab can be populated with assets of your choice by using an Asset Browser.

The Asset Browser

The Asset Browser lets you browse by asset category and Asset Pack (Pack Files), as well as search (by tag) for assets. Once displayed, the asset can be selected for inclusion in the Assets tab. See **Browsing** (next page) for more information.

The Asset Manager

Use the **Asset Manager** to create your own Asset Packs by using assets from other Asset Packs and/or by importing pictures, graphics, or backgrounds. You can tag assets and then save or export your custom asset pack. See Creating custom Asset Packs in PagePlus Help.

Browsing

The **Asset Browser** offers a whole range of professional ready-to-go designs that you can use directly in your publication. These designs are provided in categorized Asset Packs installed with PagePlus. You can browse these packs and preview their contents, before adding assets to your workspace.

There are two ways to browse assets—by category or by Asset Pack. You can also use the search controls at the top-right of the dialog to narrow your search, or to find a specific asset.

To browse assets (by category):

1.   From the Assets tab, click **Browse**.

2.   In the **Asset Browser**, select an asset category from the **Categories** section. You'll see installed Asset Packs appear in the main pane, stored under their Pack file names, e.g. Arctic.

3.   Scroll through the asset packs to browse assets included in each pack.

To browse assets (by Asset Pack):

1.   From the Assets tab, click **Browse**.

2.   In the **Asset Browser**, on the left-hand side of the dialog, select an asset pack name from the **Pack Files** section, e.g., Backgrounds. The Asset Pack will appear in the main pane.

3.   The assets are categorized further in the main pane by the name of the Asset Pack to which they belong, e.g., Fun. Scroll through to browse the assets included in each Asset Pack. To make browsing easier, you can expand and collapse the Asset Packs to hide or reveal the assets.

4. (Optional) To narrow your search, **filter** assets by entering an asset name in the **Search** box at the top-right of the main pane.

Adding assets to your Assets tab

To add a specific asset:

- Select the **category** or **pack file** in the Asset Browser, and then simply click the asset. A check mark shows on the thumbnail.

To add all assets:

- Click **Add All** from the upper-right corner of each Asset Pack's thumbnail gallery. Check marks will show on all thumbnails.

With either method, asset(s) will be available to you from the Assets tab when you close the Asset Browser.

Adding assets to your page

To add an asset to the page:

- Click an asset's thumbnail in your chosen category and drag it onto the page.

Text

5

Understanding text frames

Typically, text in PagePlus goes into **text frames**, which work equally well as containers for single words, standalone paragraphs, multipage articles, or chapter text.

 You can also use artistic text (see p. 57) for standalone text with special effects, or table text for row-and-column displays.

What's a text frame?

A text frame is a container (like a mini-page) in which the main text for your publication is stored; in PagePlus, the text in the frame is actually called a **story**.

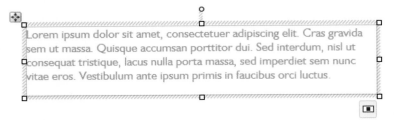

The text frame can be sized and positioned in advance of, or after, adding body text. When you move a text frame, its story text moves with it. When you resize a text frame, its story text reflows to the new dimensions.

Perhaps the most important feature of text frames is the ability to flow text between linked text frames on the same or different pages. See **Linking text frames** and **Flowing text through frames** on p. 53 and 51.

For now we'll look at a text frame as an object and the frame text contained within a single frame.

Creating text frames

You add text frames and position them on the page as you would any other object, in advance of adding text content.

1. Select **Standard Text Frame** on the **Tools** toolbar.

2. Click on the page or pasteboard to create a new frame at a default size.

    - or -

    Drag out to place the text frame at your chosen dimensions.

To delete a frame:

*   Select the frame—click its edge until a solid border appears—and then press the **Delete** key.

You can select, move, and resize text frames just like other objects (see PagePlus Help for details). When you select a frame's bounding box, indicated by a solid border, you can manage the frame properties; selecting inside a frame creates a blinking insertion point in the frame's text (the frame's boundary box becomes hatched to indicate editing mode). In this mode, you can edit the text. (For details, see **Editing text on the page** on p. 58.)

Putting text into a frame

You can put text into a frame using one of the following methods:

WritePlus story editor:	With a selected frame, click **Edit story in WritePlus** on the Frame context toolbar.
Importing text:	Select the frame, then select **Text File** from the **Insert** menu.

Typing into the frame:	Select the Pointer Tool, then click for an insertion point to type text straight into a frame, or edit existing text. (See **Editing text on the page** on p. 58.)
Pasting via the Clipboard:	At an insertion point in the text, press **Ctrl+V**.
Drag and drop:	Select text (e.g. in a word processor file), then drag it onto the PagePlus page.

Frame linking

Text frames can stand alone or they can be linked so that a single story continues from one frame to another. In any publication, you can create text in a single frame, spread a story over several linked frames, or include as many independent and linked frames as you like. By placing text frames anywhere, in any order, you can build up newspaper or newsletter style publications with a story flowing:

- between linked frames on the same page.

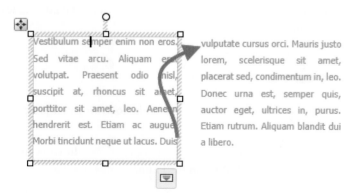

- between linked frames on different pages.

- from one column to another in the same frame.

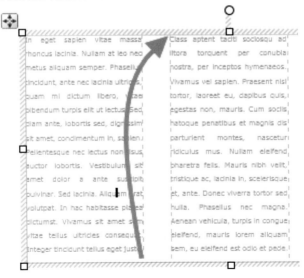

Frame properties and layout

The **frame layout** controls how text will flow in the frame. The frame can contain multiple **columns**. When a frame is selected, its column margins appear as dashed grey guide lines if set in **Frame Properties**. Note that unlike the page margin and row/column guides, which serve as layout guides for placing page elements, the frame column guides actually determine how text flows within each frame. Text won't flow outside the column margins.

You can drag the column guides or use a dialog to adjust the top and bottom **column blinds** and the left and right **column margins**.

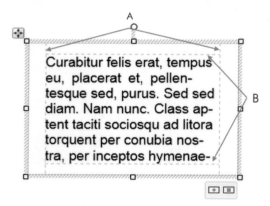

*(**A**) Column margins, (**B**) Column blinds.*

To edit frame properties directly:

- Select the frame object, then drag column guide lines to adjust the boundaries of the column.

| (1) | (2) | (3) |

The frame edge is clicked to show a **selected** bounding box (**1**), after dragging inwards the column margin can be adjusted (**2**), and after dragging downwards, the top margin blind can be moved (**3**).

To edit frame properties using a dialog:

1. Select the frame and click 🖼 **Text Frame Properties** on the Frame context toolbar.

2. From the dialog, use the three menu options to set up your frame.

    *   **General**: precisely define frame padding and column margins (**Left** and **Right**), enable/disable text wrapping around an object, and enable/disable the Auto-frame feature. (See **Wrapping text** and **Flowing text through frames** on p. 64 and 51, respectively.)

    *   **Columns**: set the **Number of columns**, and, for each column set the column **Width**, Column Blinds (**Top**, **Bottom**), **Gutter** distance between columns, and if you want to apply column **Rules** between columns. To change any value, click a column cell in the table and enter a new value.

    *   **Baseline grid**: enable a **Baseline grid** for your frame text.

3. Click **OK**.

To apply the same values across all columns in the dialog, hover over a column header, then select 'Make Values Equal', 'Set Values to Lowest', or 'Set Values to Highest' using the drop-down menu.

Adding pictures into a text frame

Pictures can be placed inline at any point in your story in a text frame, with PagePlus prompting you to resize the picture to fit with the text frames dimensions if it is too large.

If you add further story text before the picture, the inline picture will move with the surrounding text.

To add a picture to a text frame:

1. Add an empty paragraph to your text frame at the point you want to add your picture, i.e. press Return at the end of a paragraph.

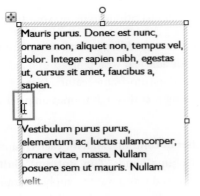

2. From the **Picture** flyout on the **Tools** toolbar, click **Import Picture**.

3. Navigate to your picture, select it and click **Open**.

4. If the picture dimensions exceed those of the text frame, click **Yes** in the displayed dialog to scale down the picture.

Flowing text through frames

If you have more text than will fit in one text frame, you have the following options to accommodate the text:

- Shrink the text to fit the frame

- Manually create and link multiple frames (p. 53)

- Use AutoFlow to automatically create new frames (p. 55)

- Use Auto-frame to dynamically, continually add or remove text frames (p. 56)

Fitting text to frames

Once frames are in position it's still possible to control how text is distributed throughout the frame(s) via tools on the Frame context toolbar.

A ⏷ The **Text Sizing** flyout offers three tools for controlling how frame text scales through the text frame. These are "one-off" operations (compared to the "continuous" **Autofit** options shown below).

A Fit Text

Click to scale the story's text size so it fits exactly into the available frame(s); further text added to the frame will cause text overflow. You can use this early on, to gauge how the story fits, or near the end, to apply the finishing touch. Fit Text first applies small point size changes, then small leading changes, then adjustments to the paragraph space below value, until the text fits.

Enlarge Text

Click to increase the story's text size one increment (approx. 2%).

 Shrink Text

Click to reduce the story's text size one increment (approx. 2%).

Each frame's story text can adopt its own individual autofit setting as follows:

 The **AutoFit Options** flyout offers three autofit options which continuously act upon a selected frame's story text.

 No AutoFit

This is the normal mode of operation where, if selected, text won't automatically scale throughout the selected text frame, possibly leaving partly empty frames at the end of the frame sequence.

 Shrink Text on Overflow

If selected, extra text added to a selected frame will shrink all frame text to avoid text overflow.

 AutoFit

If selected, the frame will always scale text automatically by adjusting text size (compare to **Fit Text** which fits text once, with any additional text causing text overflow).

 Auto-Frame

If selected, whenever overflowing frame text occurs, additional pages are created containing same-sized text frames which dynamically populate with the overflowing text.

Linking text frames

When a text frame is selected, the frame includes a **Link** button at the bottom right which denotes the state of the frame and its story text. It also allows you to control how the frame's story flows to following frames:

No Overflow
The frame is not linked to a following frame (it's either a standalone frame or the last frame in a sequence) and the frame is empty or the end of the story text is visible.

Overflow
The populated frame is not linked (either standalone or last frame) and there is additional story text in the **hidden** overflow area.

An **Autoflow** button also appears to the left of the **Link** button.

Continued
The frame is linked to a following frame. The end of the story text may be visible, or it may flow into the following frame.

> The button icon will be red if the final frame of the sequence is overflowing, or green if there's no overflow.

There are two basic ways to set up a linked sequence of frames:

- You can link a sequence of empty frames, then import the text.

- You can import the text into a single frame, then create and link additional frames into which the text automatically flows.

> When frames are created by the **AutoFlow** option (for example when importing text), they are automatically linked in sequence.

To create a link or reorder the links between existing frames, you can use the **Link** button under the frame. Remember to watch the cursor, which changes to indicate these operations.

- You can link to frames already containing text or are already in a link sequence.

- If the frame was not part of a link sequence, its text is merged into the selected text's story.

To link the selected frame to an existing frame:

1. Click the frame's **Link** button (showing ▣ or ▣ .)

2. Click with the Textflow cursor on the frame to be linked to.

To link the selected frame to a newly drawn frame:

- As above, but instead of clicking a "target" frame, either click on the page (for a default frame) or drag across the page (to create a frame sized to your requirements). The latter is ideal for quickly mapping out linked frames across different pages.

To unlink the selected frame from the sequence:

- Click on ▣ **Continued**, then click with the Textflow cursor on the same frame.

Story text remains with the "old" frames. For example, if you detach the second frame of a three-frame sequence, the story text remains in the first and third frames, which are now linked into a two-frame story. The detached frame is always empty.

AutoFlow

If your text frames are not set to Auto-frame (see p. 56) and there's too much story text to fit in a frame sequence, PagePlus stores it in an invisible **overflow area**. To indicate this overflow, the Link button on the last frame of the sequence displays 🔲 and an 🔳 **AutoFlow** button appears next to it. The **AutoFlow** feature will automatically flow text into available, empty text frames, or create text frames on new pages, for you.

To AutoFlow story text on the page:

- Click the 🔳 **AutoFlow** button just to the left of the frame's 🔲 **Link** button.

  - If an empty frame exists anywhere in your publication, PagePlus will detect the first empty frame and prompt to flow text into this. Click **Yes** to flow into frame or click **No** to let PagePlus detect and jump to the next empty frame.

  - If no other empty frames are detected, you'll be prompted to autoflow text into a new frame(s) the same size as the original or to new frame(s) sized to the page.

AutoFlow is a "one-off" operation compared to the "continuous" Auto-frame option described on p. 56. If you add more text to a story while editing, or have reduced the size of a frame, you may find that an overflow condition crops up. In this case you can decide whether to click the frame's **AutoFlow** button again or use a **text sizing option**. If you reduce the amount of text in the story, empty frames will remain on the page.

Automatic text frame creation using Auto-frame

Auto-frame is an option which can be set on any frame in your publication. Once this is set, PagePlus will automatically create new text frames on new pages if there is too much content to fill the initial frame. Furthermore, it will automatically remove empty text frames (and empty pages) if content is reduced. This, alongside WritePlus, could be considered PagePlus's 'word processing mode'.

To switch on Auto-frame:

- With a text frame selected, on the context toolbar, from the **AutoFit Options** flyout, select **Auto-frame**.

Now, when additional content is added to this text frame which would otherwise overflow the frame, a new text frame of identical size is created containing this additional content. By default, this new frame is added to a newly created page but this behaviour can be modified (see PagePlus Help for details).

Conversely, if content is removed from the sequence of text frames to leave an empty frame, this empty frame is removed along with the page it resides on (unless additional content is present on the page).

Using artistic text

Artistic text is standalone text you type directly onto a page. Especially useful for headlines, pull quotes, and other special-purpose text, it's easily formatted with the standard text tools.

To create artistic text:

1.   Choose the **A** **Artistic Text Tool** from the **Tools** toolbar.

2.   Click on the page to make an insertion point from where you'll begin typing.

3.   Set initial text properties (style, font, point size, etc.) using the Text context toolbar.

4.   Start typing to create the artistic text using your chosen text properties.

Once you've created an artistic text object, you can select, move, resize, delete, and copy it just as you would with a text frame. **Solid colours**, **gradient/bitmap fills**, and **transparency** can all be applied.

To resize or reproportion an artistic text object:

*   To resize while maintaining the object's proportions, drag the resize handles.

*   To resize freely, hold down the **Shift** key while dragging.

To edit artistic text:

*   Drag to select a range of text, creating a blue selection.

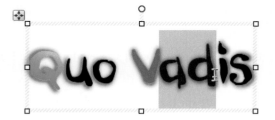

You can double- or triple-click to select a word or all text.

Now you can type new text, apply **character and paragraph formatting**, edit the text in WritePlus, apply proofing options, and so on.

Editing text on the page

You can use the Pointer Tool to edit **frame text**, **table text**, or **artistic text** directly. On the page, you can select and enter text, set paragraph indents and tab stops, change text properties, and apply text styles.

Selecting and entering text

The selection of frame text, artistic text, and table text follows the conventions of the most up-to-date word-processing tools. The selection area is shaded in semi-transparent blue for clear editing.

Nulla **vestibulum** eleifend
nulla. Suspendisse potenti.
Aliquam turpis nisi, venenatis
non, accum san nec, imperdiet
laoreet, lacus.

Double-, triple- or quadruple-click selects a word, paragraph or all text, respectively. You can also make use of the **Ctrl**-click or drag for selection of non-adjacent words, the **Shift** key for ranges of text.

To edit text on the page:

1. Select the Pointer Tool, then click (or drag) in the text object. A standard insertion point appears at the click position (see below),
    - or -
    Select a single word, paragraph or portion of text.

2. Type to insert new text or overwrite selected text, respectively.

Nulla vestibulum eleifend
nulla. Suspendisse potenti.
Aliquam turpis nisi, venenatis
non, accum san nec, imperdiet
laoreet, lacus.

To start a new paragraph:

- Press the Return key.

To start a new line within the same paragraph (using a line break or soft return):

- Press **Shift**+Return.

To flow text to the next column (Column Break), frame (Frame Break) or page (Page Break):

- Press **Ctrl**+Return, **Alt**+Return or **Ctrl+Shift**+Return, respectively.

The first two options apply only to frame text. You can use these shortcuts or choose the items from the **Insert>Break** submenu.

To switch between insert mode and overwrite mode:

- Press the **Insert** key.

Checking your text

To ensure your artistic and frame text is error-free and the best copy possible, use the **Spell Checker**, **Proof Reader**, and **Thesaurus** options on the **Tools** menu.

For paragraph indents and tab stops, see PagePlus Help or consider applying indents and tab stops as body text styles (p. 61).

Setting text properties

PagePlus gives you a high degree of typographic control over characters and paragraphs, whether you're working with **frame text**, **table text**, or **artistic text**.

To apply basic text formatting:

1. Select the text.

2. Use buttons on the Text context toolbar to change text style, font, point size, attributes, paragraph alignment, bullets/numbering, or level.

| Body | ▾ | Gill Sans MT | ▾ | 12 pt | ▾ | **B** *I* <u>U</u> ▾ | *O* ▾ | ≡ ≡ ≡ ≡ |

To apply paragraph formatting:

*   From the Paragraph tab, select options to control paragraph-level alignment, indent, line spacing, auto-hyphenation, and alignment to baseline grid.

To clear local formatting (restore plain/default text properties):

1. Select a range of text with local formatting.

2. Click on the **Clear Formatting** option on the Text context toolbar's text styles drop-down list (or Text Styles tab).

Using text styles

PagePlus lets you use named **text styles** (pre-defined or user-defined), which can be applied to **frame text**, **table text**, **artistic text**, index text or table of contents text. A text style is a set of character and/or paragraph attributes saved as a group. When you apply a style to text, you apply the whole group of attributes in just one step. For example, you could use named paragraph styles for particular layout elements, such as "Heading 1" or "Body", and character styles to convey meaning, such as "Emphasis", "Strong", or "Subtle Reference".

Styles can be applied to characters or paragraphs using either the Text context toolbar or the Text Styles tab. Both paragraph and character styles can be managed from the **Text Style Palette**.

Paragraph and character styles

A **paragraph style** is a complete specification for the appearance of a paragraph, including all font and paragraph format attributes. Every paragraph in PagePlus has a paragraph style associated with it.

A **character style** includes only font attributes (name, point size, bold, italic, etc.), and you apply it at the character level—that is, to a range of selected characters—rather than to the whole paragraph.

Working with named styles

Body ▾ The named style of the currently selected text is displayed in either the **Text Styles** tab or the **Styles** drop-down list on the Text context toolbar. A character style (if one is applied locally) may be shown; otherwise it indicates the paragraph style.

To apply a named style:

1. Using the Pointer Tool, click in a paragraph (if applying a paragraph style) or select a range of text (if applying a character style).

2. Display the **Text Styles** tab and select a style from the style list.
    - or -
    On the Text context toolbar, click the arrow to expand the Styles drop-down list and select a style name.

The Text Style tab highlights the paragraph or character style applied to any selected text.

As both paragraph and character formatting can be applied to the same text, all of the current text's formatting is displayed in the **Current format** box on the tab. In the example below, currently selected text has a 'Strong' character style applied over a 'Body' paragraph style.

Current format: Body + Strong

To update a named style using the properties of existing text:

1. Make your desired formatting changes to any text that uses a named style.

2. On the **Text Styles** tab, right-click the style and choose **Update <style> to Match Selection**.

All text using the named style, throughout the publication, takes on the new properties.

To modify an existing style:

- From the Text Styles tab, right-click on the character or paragraph style you want to modify and then choose **Modify <style>.**

Creating custom text styles

If required, you can create your own custom styles, either based on a currently selected text style or from scratch. See PagePlus Help for more information.

Wrapping text

PagePlus lets you wrap frame text around the contours of a separate object. Usually, this means wrapping text to a picture that overlaps or sits above a text frame. But you can wrap frame text around a shape, artistic text, table, or another frame. Wrapping is accomplished by changing the **wrap setting** for the object to which text will wrap.

Vestibulum semper enim non eros. Sed vitae arcu. Aliquam erat volutpat. Praesent odio nisl, suscipit at, rhoncus sit amet, porttitor sit amet, leo. Aenean hendrerit est. Etiam ac augue. Morbi tincidunt neque ut lacus. Duis vulputate cursus orci. Mauris justo lorem, scelerisque sit amet, placerat sed, condimentum in, leo. Donec urna est, semper quis, auctor eget, ultrices in, purus. Etiam rutrum.

To wrap text around an object:

1. Select the object around which you want the text to wrap.

2. Click the 🔲 **Wrap Settings** button on the **Arrange** toolbar.

3. Select the manner in which text will wrap around the object by clicking a sample.

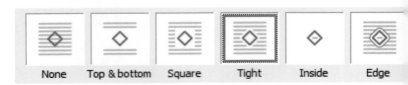

4. Choose which side(s) the chosen wrapping method will be applied, again by clicking a sample.

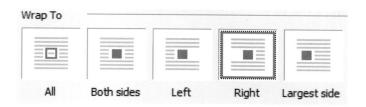

The examples show tight wrapping applied to the right of the object only.

5. Click **OK**.

You can manually adjust the wrap outline using the Curve context toolbar for more precise text fitting.

Creating a bulleted or numbered list

You can turn a series of paragraphs into **bulleted**, **numbered** or **multi-level lists**. Bullets are especially useful when listing items of interest in no specific order of preference, numbered lists for presenting step-by-step procedures (by number or letter), and multi-level lists for more intelligent hierarchical lists with prefixed numbers, symbols, or a mix of both, all with supporting optional text.

Bulleted list   *Numbered list*   *Multi-level list*

Lists can be applied to normal text (as local formatting) or to **text styles** equally.

To create a simple bulleted or numbered list:

1. Select one or more paragraphs.
    - or -
    Click in a paragraph's text.

2. Select ☰ **Bulleted List** or ☷ **Numbered List** from the Text context toolbar.

To create a bulleted or numbered list (using presets):

1. Select one or more paragraphs.
    - or -
    Click in a paragraph's text.

2. Select **Bullets and Numbering** from the **Format** menu.

3. From the Text Style dialog's Bullets and Numbering menu option, choose **Bullet**, **Number**, or **Multi-Level** from the **Style** drop-down list.

4. Select one of the preset formats shown by default.
    - or -
    For a custom list, click the **Details** button to display, then alter custom options.

5. Click **OK** to apply list formatting.

> For number and multi-level lists, check **Restart numbering** to restart numbering from the current cursor position in the list; otherwise, leave the option unchecked.

> Turn off list formatting by clicking the Text context toolbar's ☰ or ☷ buttons again.

Tables, Charts, and Calendars

6

Creating tables

Tables are ideal for presenting text and data in a variety of easily customizable row-and-column formats, with built-in spreadsheet capabilities.

	J	F	M	A	M	J	J	A	S	O	N	D
N	12	8	7	9	11	8	18	11	3	11	22	16
S	6	6	7	10	9	12	11	13	7	13	14	10
W	12	6	5	20	9	18	17	14	10	14	13	18

Rather than starting from scratch, PagePlus is supplied with a selection of pre-defined table formats, called **AutoFormats**, that can be used. Simply pick one and fill in the cells with content.

PagePlus lets you:

- Edit the pre-defined format before adding a new table to the page.

- Design your own custom formats without creating a table. See Creating custom table formats in PagePlus Help.

- Quickly create custom formats based on the selected table.

- Edit existing tables to fit a different format (pre-defined or custom).

Creating tables from scratch

To create a table:

1. On the **Tools** toolbar, choose the **Table Tool** from the **Table** flyout.

2. Click on the page or pasteboard, or drag to set the table's dimensions. The **Create Table** dialog opens with a selection of preset table formats shown in the **Format** window.

3. Step through the list to preview the layouts and select one. To begin with a plain table, select (**Default**).

4. Set the **Table Size**. This is the number of rows and columns that make up the table layout.

5. Click **OK**. The new table appears on the page.

Plan your table layout in advance, considering the number of rows/columns needed!

Creating tables from frame text

PagePlus lets you convert text within a text frame into a table. The feature is a quick way to repurpose table text copied from tables in word processing documents or web pages.

You can control the number of columns created, the cell autofit behaviour, and how text should be separated into columns and rows (depending on the type of text delimitation).

To create a table from text:

1. Select the text frame or text within the frame for conversion of all containing frame text or just selected regions of text, respectively.

2. From the **Table** menu, select **Create Table from Selection**.

Using charts

For any small business, club, or school project, the ability to present important data professionally will impress your audience and potentially gain support for your activities.

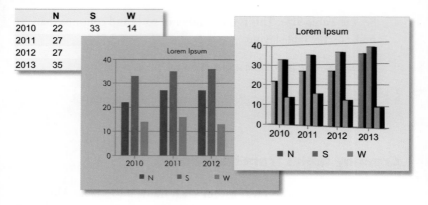

	N	S	W
2010	22	33	14
2011	27		
2012	27		
2013	35		

Tables and charts are intrinsically linked in PagePlus. If you need a recap on tables, see **Creating tables** on p. 68. PagePlus also lets you create multiple charts from the same table data using the **Chart Data** tab. See Manipulating chart data (in PagePlus Help) for more information.

Chart types

PagePlus provides a range of popular chart types, each designed to present data differently. All you need to do is select a chart that suits the type of data you wish to present.

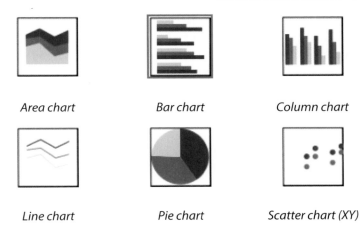

Area chart   *Bar chart*   *Column chart*

Line chart   *Pie chart*   *Scatter chart (XY)*

Creating charts from scratch

PagePlus provides the **Chart Tool** to place a chart onto your page.
Initially a placeholder chart, it can be populated with real chart data
from the **Chart Data** tab. The tab lets you store and develop your chart
data "off-page" without cluttering up your page design.

The chart can be designed and later modified by using a Chart context
toolbar displayed above your workspace when the chart is selected.

To create a chart from scratch:

1. From the **Tools** toolbar's **Table Tools** flyout,
    select **Chart Tool**.

2. On the context toolbar, from the **Chart** drop-down list, select a
    chart type.

3. Click on the page or drag out the chart to the desired size.

At this point, the chart is just a placeholder, using sample data automatically added to the **Chart Data** tab. You can edit this sample data using your own data, name your row/column headers, and even add extra rows and columns to suit additional chart data—by default, each row represents a separate colour-coded series component.

To edit data in the Chart Data tab:

1.   Click **Chart Data** under the selected chart. The Chart Data tab displays temporarily in the workspace.

2.   On the **Chart Data** tab, click in each cell and enter data as appropriate. The chart will update with the newly entered values.

3.   Replace the row and numeric column headers (i.e., Series 1, 2, and 3; and 1, 2, 3, 4, respectively) with real names. These will update in your chart immediately.

Modifying charts

It is possible that you may want to change how your chart is presented. The Chart context toolbar gives you the freedom to swap between chart types, base your chart on different ranges, and toggle series as row or columns.

Formatting and styling charts

The **Charts** tab serves a dual purpose in PagePlus—to fine tune the chart's look and to manage how the series are used in your chart. In addition, the **Styles** tab can be used to apply a completely new look to your chart in one go, even swapping the chart type.

To display the Charts tab:

- At the bottom of your right-hand tab group, click **Charts**.

The tab offers three buttons called Chart, Axes, and Series.

- **Chart**: Used for title and series legend control and positioning. Other options are the same as provided on the Chart context toolbar.

- **Axes**: The Axes section adds axis-specific titles, labels, guides, and any other chart elements that aid the interpretation of chart data.

- **Series**: Modifies individual series, including manually assigning series labels, series plotting, enabling trendlines, error bars, and value labels.

Inserting a calendar

The **Calendar Wizard** helps you design month-at-a-glance calendars for use in your publication, with optional addition of personal events and public holidays.

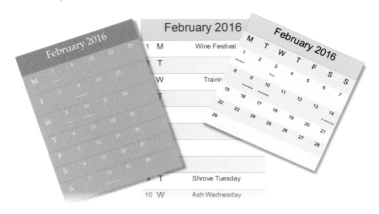

The calendar is created as a scalable **text-based table** so you can edit text using the standard text tools. The properties of a selected calendar are similar to those of a table, and can be modified identically (see Manipulating tables in PagePlus Help). Like custom table formats you can create your own custom calendar formats.

To insert a calendar:

1. Click the Table flyout on the **Tools** toolbar and choose **Insert Calendar**.

2. Click again on your page, or drag out to set the desired size of the calendar.

3. From the displayed **Calendar Wizard**, define options for your calendar including setting the year and month, calendar style (square, or in single or double column format), week start day, room to write, display options, and calendar format.

4. Click **Finish** to complete the wizard.

To view and edit a selected calendar's properties:

- Click **Edit Calendar** on the Calendar context toolbar.

Adding calendar events

March 2016	
1 T	St. David's Day
2 W	
3 T	
4 F	
5 S	
6 S	
7 M	Wellbeing Conference
8 T	International Womens Day
9 W	Cassie's Birthday

You can add events to your calendar by using the **Calendar Event Manager**; click the **Calendar Events** button on a selected calendar's context toolbar to access.

The Calendar Event Manager adds events to a month-to-view calendar display. They show automatically on your calendar under the chosen date and with a colour code that indicates the calendar category. New categories have unique colours assigned to them on creation.

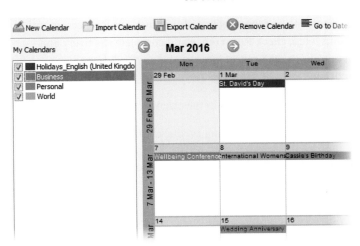

Instead of recreating a calendar from scratch you can import existing iCalendar files (*.ics) plus other calendar file formats that already contain events. Exporting your calendars to an iCalendar file is also possible.

To create a calendar:

1. From the Calendar Event Manager, click ![icon] **New Calendar** on the top toolbar. A new calendar entry (named 'New Calendar 1, 2, 3, etc.) appears in the My Calendars box.

2. Type a name for the calendar (e.g., 'Business') and press Return.

To add an event to the selected calendar:

1. Navigate to a chosen month in your calendar using the month navigator at the top of the calendar, then double-click the event day.

2. Enter your event text into the text input box. This displays in your calendar under the chosen date.

3. (Optional) Use the **Calendar** drop-down list, to choose which category in which to store your event, e.g. in Business.

4. If the event is to be repeating (e.g., for annual conferences, monthly payments, etc.), check **Recurrence** and complete the Every and Until options to set a repeat interval and any end date as appropriate.

5. Click **OK**. The event appears in the calendar under the chosen date.

6. When you have finished adding events, click **Close**.

> The Calendar Event Manager lets you display public holidays which are automatically set up for your current location. Simply check the box on the holiday category.

To modify an event:

•   Double click the event on the calendar.

To switch on calendars:

•   Check the calendar entry in the My Calendars window.

Pictures

Adding picture frames

Picture frames let you present your pictures in a decorative surround,
much like you'd show off your favourite picture in a picture frame in
your home. You can select from an impressive collection of
professionally designed picture frames, and simply drag them onto your
publication page before filling them with pictures.

Picture frames are **assets**, along with graphics, pictures, page elements,
backgrounds, and are **browsed for** (and managed) in the same way as
any other asset. See **Using assets** on p. 38.

To add a picture frame:

1.   From the Assets tab, select **Browse**.

2.   In the **Asset Browser** dialog, select **Picture Frames** from the
     Categories section.

3. Navigate the themed sub-categories to locate a picture frame, then select an individual frame or click **Add All** ✅ to include all the frames from the sub-category. A check mark will appear on selected thumbnails.

4. Click **Close**. The frame(s) appears in the **Assets** tab (Picture Frames category).

5. Drag a chosen frame thumbnail to your page.

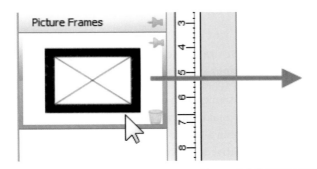

> Empty picture frames are shown as envelope-shaped placeholders on the page.

To add a borderless picture frame:

1. ⬚ ▭ ▾ Select **Rectangular Picture Frame** on the **Tools** toolbar's **Picture** flyout.

   - or -

   Select **Picture>Empty Frame** from the **Insert** menu.

2. ▦ The mouse pointer changes to the **Picture Paste** cursor. What you do next determines the initial size and placement of the picture frame.

   • To insert the frame at a default size, simply click the mouse.

     - or -

- To set the size of the frame, drag out a region and release the mouse button. If needed, use the **Shift** key while dragging to maintain aspect ratio (to a square).

> Picture frames can also be applied to objects such as text frames and tables.

To add a picture to a frame (and vice versa):

- From the Assets tab (Pictures category), drag and drop a picture directly onto the picture frame.

  - or -

- From the Assets tab (Picture Frames category), drag and drop a picture frame directly onto an already placed picture.

The picture is added to the frame using default Picture Frame properties, i.e. it is scaled to maximum fit; aspect ratio is always maintained. However, you can alter the picture's size, orientation, positioning, and scaling relative to its frame using the button shown under the selected frame or Frame Properties on the Picture context toolbar.

Creating shaped picture frames

While you can take advantage of PagePlus's preset frames you can create your own shape (e.g., a morphed QuickShape or closed curve) then convert it to a picture frame.

To create a shaped picture frame:

1. Create a closed shape or QuickShape.

2. Right-click the shape and select **Convert To>Picture Frame**.

You can then add a picture to the frame as described previously.

To store the picture frame for reuse globally or just in the publication, drag to the Assets tab's My Designs or Picture Frames category. For the latter, if you close the publication, you'll be asked if you want to save the frame to an asset pack. See Storing designs in PagePlus Help.

Adding pictures

The **Assets** tab (Pictures category) acts as a "basket" for initially gathering together and then including pictures in your publication. Its chief use is to aid the design process by improving efficiency (avoiding having to import pictures one by one) and convenience (making pictures always-at-hand). For picture-rich publications in particular, the tab is a valuable tool for dragging pictures directly into **bordered** or **unbordered** picture frames or for simply replacing existing pictures on the page.

PagePlus also lets you insert pictures of a wide variety of file formats, such as bitmaps, vector images, metafiles (including Serif Metafiles), and DrawPlus files.

 PDF files can also be placed as non-editable graphics. When placed as graphics, PDFs be moved, rotated, cropped and recoloured like normal images, but cannot be edited using PhotoLab, the Cutout Studio, or an external image editing program. To edit PDFs in PagePlus they need to be opened or inserted as editable documents.

For photos from your digital camera, you can simply navigate to the folder containing your already downloaded photos (i.e., on your hard disk) and include them in the tab. Similarly, scanned images already saved to your hard disk can be added by this method.

Adding pictures to the Assets tab

To add pictures to the tab:

1. Select the Assets tab's Pictures category, and click **Add.**

2. From the dialog, navigate to a folder, and select your picture(s).

3. Click **Open**. Your pictures appear as thumbnails within the Assets tab's Picture category.

Adding pictures to the page

Pictures can be added to your publication from the Assets tab by dragging directly onto your page.

Adding pictures with resizing and embed/link control

As well as dragging a picture thumbnail from the Assets tab, pictures can be added to PagePlus by copy and paste or dragging a file from an external Windows folder directly onto your page.

PagePlus also lets you import pictures via **Import Picture** on the **Tools** toolbar. You'll be able to size the picture and embed/link the picture in your publication.

You can use this method to place DrawPlus X8 project files (*.dpp) directly on your PagePlus page.

Cropping pictures

PagePlus includes the **Square Crop Tool** and **Irregular Crop Tool** which are used typically for cropping pictures on the page. Cropping discards unwanted "outer" regions of a picture while keeping the remainder visible.

To crop a picture (square crop):

1. ⬜ Select a picture and then on the **Attributes** toolbar, click the **Square Crop Tool**.

2. Hover over an edge or corner handle until you see a ⊞ crop cursor appear.

3. Drag the cursor inwards (down, left or right) on your picture.

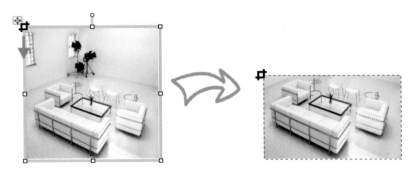

4. Repeat with other edge or corner handles, if needed.

5. (Optional) From the context toolbar, set a **Feather** value to add a soft edge to your picture.

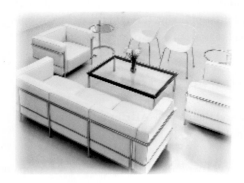

To crop a picture (irregular crop)

1. With the ⧄ **Square Crop Tool** selected, select the ◱ **Irregular Crop Tool** above your workspace.

2. The Curve context toolbar appears on its right, which lets you control the displayed nodes and connecting segments that define the object's crop outline.

- To move a node (control point) where you see the ⁻ı⁻ cursor, drag the node.

- ↖︎∪ To move a line segment (between two nodes) where you see the cursor, drag the segment.

3. Add extra nodes by double-clicking on the crop outline, then reposition them.

To scale the object within the crop outline, press the **Ctrl** key, click your left mouse button, then move your mouse upwards or downwards.

If you add **picture frames** to your publication, you can position your placed picture using pan and zoom instead of using the Square Crop Tool.

Cropping pictures to shapes

The **Crop to Shape** command lets you create shaped pictures from drawn closed shapes (below) or silhouettes placed over your picture. The picture gets clipped to the outline of the shape, leaving a shape equivalent to the overlapping region.

To crop a picture using shapes:

1. Place the shape in front of the picture to be cropped, using the **Arrange** menu and/or **Arrange** toolbar as needed.

2. With both objects selected (or grouped), choose **Crop to Shape** from the **Tools** menu.

You can restore an object cropped in this way to its original shape, but the upper "cropping" object is permanently deleted (use **Undo** to recover it if necessary).

Using Cutout Studio

Cutout Studio offers a powerful integrated solution for cutting objects out from their backgrounds.

The initial green background is discarded, from which another image can be used as a more attractive background. A red tint on the second image's background is used to indicate areas to be discarded.

To launch Cutout Studio:

1. Select a picture to be cut out.

2. Select **Cutout Studio** from the displayed Picture context toolbar. Cutout Studio is launched.

Choose an output

By default an alpha-edged bitmap is created by cutting out, but's possible to change the **Output Type** prior to selecting areas for keeping/discarding.

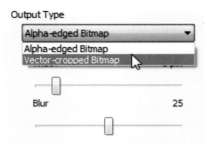

The choice you make really depends on the picture. A vector-edged bitmap is better for cutting out pictures with well defined edges.

Selecting areas to keep or discard

A pair of brushes for keeping and discarding is used to "paint" areas of the image. The tools are called **Keep Brush** and **Discard Brush**, and are either used independently or, more typically, in combination with each other.

To select image areas for keeping/discarding:

1.   In Cutout Studio, click either **Keep Brush Tool** or **Discard Brush Tool** from the left of the Studio workspace.

2.   (Optional) Pick a **Brush size** suitable for the area to be worked on.

3.   (Optional) Set a **Grow Tolerance** value to automatically expand the selected area under the cursor (by detecting colours similar to those within the current selection). The greater the value the more the selected area will grow. Uncheck the option to switch the feature off.

4.   Using the circular cursor, click and drag across the area to be retained or discarded (depending on Keep or Discard Brush Tool

selection). It's OK to repeatedly click and drag until your selection area is made.

The  **Undo** button reverts to the last made selection.

5. If you're outputting an alpha-edged bitmap, you can refine the area to be kept/discarded within Cutout Studio (only after previewing) with Erase and Restore **touch-up tools**. Vector-cropped images can be cropped using standard PagePlus crop tools outside of the Studio.

6. Click  **OK** to create your cutout.

Use  **Restore** or  **Erase Touch-up** tools for fine-tuning your alpha-edged bitmap after preview.

PhotoLab filters and retouching tools

PhotoLab is a powerful studio for applying adjustment and effect filters to pictures individually or in combination—all instantly applied and previewed—and carrying out popular edits like image straightening!

PhotoLab hosts filter tabs, a main toolbar, and applied filter stack around a central workspace.

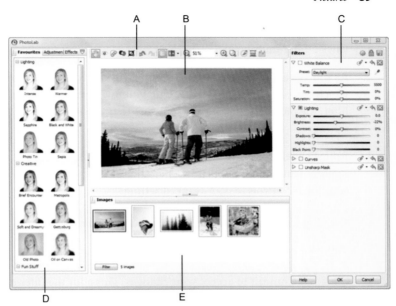

(**A**) *Main toolbar,* (**B**) *Main workspace,* (**C**) *Filter stack,* (**D**) *Filter tabs,*
(**E**) *Images tab*

To launch PhotoLab:

1. Select the picture that you want to apply a filter to.

2. Click ⊙ **PhotoLab** on the Picture context toolbar.

Applying a filter

Filters are stored in PhotoLab's Favourites, Adjustments, and Effects
tabs which group filters logically into categories (e.g., Quick Fix for fast
and commonly used correction filters).

The Favourites tab offers some commonly used filters (individual and
in combination).

To preview, fine tune, and apply a filter:

1.   Click a filter thumbnail.

2.   As soon as a filter is selected it is temporarily added to **Trial Zone** which lets you experiment freely with your own settings for that filter; the picture automatically refreshes to preview your new settings.

3.   Adjust sliders (or enter input values) until your filter suits your requirements. Some filters offer check boxes, drop-down lists, and additional controls (e.g., Advanced settings).

Selecting a new filter always replaces the current filter.

To commit your filter:

•   Click **Commit** to accept your changes. This adds the filter to the right-most **Filters** stack where additional filters can be added and built up by using the same method.

Adjustments are applied such that the most recently added filter always appears at the bottom of the list and is applied to the picture last (after the other filters above it).

Adding QR codes

QR codes (Quick Response codes) are machine-readable matrix barcodes that can be added to your page. The QR code can be programmed to provide appropriate information or services when the code is scanned by intelligent mobile device or scanner.

To add a QR code:

1. From the **Insert** menu, select **QR Code**.

2. Click on the page at the location you want the QR code to be placed (this positions the top left corner of the QR code).

3. From the dialog's Content tab, select the **QR Code Type** by clicking a thumbnail (e.g., An Internet page). This sets the type of information to be served for the service.

4. Under the thumbnail, input data into fields or change settings as appropriate. These differ according to the QR Code Type selected.

5. Click **OK**.

Once placed, the QR Code can be sized and positioned to suit. It is recommended to maintain the code's aspect ratio to a square for best results.

To modify a QR Code:

- Using the **Pointer Tool**, double-click the QR code.

> 💡 To scan QR codes, you'll need QR Code reader software installed on your mobile device. Search for 'QR Code Reader' using your favourite search engine or download from your online software store.

QR codes and mail merge

Mail merge uses the data from a data source (e.g., a Serif Database) to populate a page area that repeats automatically per data source record, until all records are presented sequentially in a new merged publication.

You can insert a QR Code field into a repeating area by using the **Mail and Photo Merge** toolbar.

For more information, see Using mail merge in PagePlus Help.

Colour, Fills, and Transparency

8

Applying solid fills

PagePlus offers a number of ways to apply solid colour fills to objects of different kinds:

- You can apply solid colours to an object's **line** or **fill**. As you might expect, QuickShapes and closed shapes have both line and fill properties, whereas straight and freehand lines have only a line property.

- Characters in text objects can have a background fill, line, and text colour (i.e., for highlighting, text outlines, and the text fill itself). Text frames and table cells can have a background fill independent of the characters they contain.

To apply a solid colour via the Colour tab or Swatches tab:

1. Select the object(s) or highlight a range of text.

2. Select the appropriate tab, then click the **Fill**, **Line**, or **Text** button at the top of the tab to determine where colour will be applied. The colour of the underline reflects the colour of your selected object.

3. For the Colour tab, select a colour from the colour spectrum or sliders depending on colour mode selected.

   - or -

   For the Swatches tab, select a colour swatch from the **Publication palette** (commonly used colours and those previously applied to your publication) or a specific themed or standard **Palette** (supplied preset swatches).

Alternatively, use **Format>Fill** to apply colour via a dialog.

Using the **Colours** toolbar, you can reapply the last applied fill, line, or text colour and also predefine these colours for future objects. By default, the toolbar is always in view thus aiding design productivity.

To apply the last applied solid colour:

1. Select the object(s) or highlight a range of text.

2.   On the **Colours** toolbar, select the **Fill**, **Line**, or **Text** button.

To predefine colours for future objects:

- With no objects selected, click the down arrow on the toolbar's **Fill**, **Line**, or **Text** buttons and choose a colour from the menu, This is equivalent to using the Colour or Swatches tab.

To change a solid colour's shade/tint (lightness):

1. Select the object and set the correct Fill, Line or Text button in the **Colour** tab.

2. From the Colour mode drop-down list, select **Tinting**.

3. Drag the Shade/Tint slider to the left or right to darken or lighten your starting colour, respectively. You can also enter a value between -100 and 100 in the box. Entering 0 in the input box reverts to the original colour.

Adjust the 18% percentage tinting via slider or direct input to apply object tinting from the **Swatches** tab.

PagePlus automatically adds used colours to the   **Publication Palette** available in the **Swatches** tab and **Fill** dialog.

From the **Swatches** tab, you can convert any colour in your palette into a spot colour. Right-click a fill, select **Edit Fill**, then check **Spot Colour** in the dialog.

To change the current palette:

- On the **Swatches** tab, click the ◼ ▾ **Palette** button to view and adopt colours from a **Standard RGB**, **Standard CMYK**, or selection of themed palettes. Colours can be added, edited, or deleted from the Publication Palette but not from other palettes.

Replacing colours

In PagePlus, changing all instances of a regular colour in your publication is easy.

This can be very useful when you have designed a publication without using scheme colours and change your mind (or a client does) about which colours to use, altering colours without manually selecting and changing each object. This can also be of benefit when editing a PDF that requires document-wide colour changes, and when choosing to turn regular colours into scheme colours.

Replace a colour in the publication palette

1. In the Swatches tab, click the down arrow on the ◼ ▾ **Publication palette** button and select **Publication Palette**.

2. Right-click on the colour you want to replace and choose **Replace Colour** from the menu.

3. Choose the new colour using one of the many colour models, palettes, pickers, and scheme colours available in the **Colour Selector** dialog.

4. Click **OK** to apply the new colour in place of the old.

Using colour schemes

In PagePlus, a **colour scheme** is a cluster of eleven complementary colours (of which **five** are mainly used) that you can apply to specific elements in one or more publications. The **Schemes** tab displays preset schemes (displaying the five main colours) which can be selected at any point during the design process.

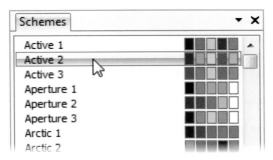

Each publication can have just one colour scheme at a time; the current scheme is highlighted in the **Schemes** tab. You can easily switch schemes, modify scheme colours and create custom schemes. Colour schemes are saved globally, so the full set of schemes is always available.

How colour schemes work

Colour schemes in PagePlus work much like a paint-by-numbers system, where various regions of a layout are coded with numbers, and a specific colour is assigned (by number) to each region.

For example, imagine a line drawing coded with the numbers 1 through 5. To fill it in, you'd use paint from jars also numbered 1 through 5. Swapping different colours into the paint jars, while keeping the numbers on the drawing the same, would produce quite a different painting.

In PagePlus, the "paint jars" are numbers you can assign to objects in your publication. They're known as "Scheme Colour 1," "Scheme Colour 2," and so on. When you apply Scheme Colour 1 to an object, it's like saying, "Put the colour from jar number 1 here."

The **Schemes** tab shows the various available schemes, each with a different set of five colours in the five "jars." Whichever named colour scheme you select, that scheme's first colour (as shown in its sample) will appear in regions defined as Scheme Colour 1, its second colour will map to Scheme Colour 2, and so on throughout the publication.

To select a colour scheme:

1. Click the **Schemes** tab. The currently assigned scheme is highlighted in the list.

2. Click a different colour scheme sample. Objects in the publication that have been assigned one of the colour scheme numbers are updated with the corresponding colour from the new scheme.

By default, the Schemes tab is collapsed at the bottom right of the workspace.

You can repeat this selection process indefinitely. When you save a publication, its current colour scheme is saved along with the document.

Applying scheme colours to objects

When you create publications from pre-defined **design templates** (see p. 12), you can choose the starting colour scheme that you want to adopt; you can always change it later from the **Schemes** tab. However, if you then create new elements in your schemed publication, or start a publication from scratch, how can you extend the current colour scheme to the new objects? Recalling the paint-by-numbers example above, all you need to do is assign one of the current scheme colour numbers to an object's line and/or fill.

To assign a scheme colour to an object:

1. On the **Swatches** tab, from the **Publications Palette** flyout, select **Scheme Colours**.

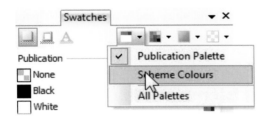

The palette displays only scheme colours.

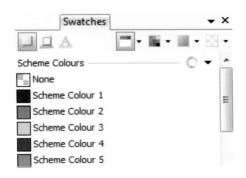

2. Select the object and choose a ▬ **Fill**, ▭ **Line**, or **A** **Text**
    button at the top of the **Swatches** tab depending on the desired
    effect.

3. Click on the scheme colour that you want to apply to the fill, line, or
    text.

If an object's fill uses a scheme colour, the corresponding sample in
Swatches tab will be highlighted whenever the object is selected.

PagePlus also allows you to modify any existing colour scheme and
create your own scheme from a colour spread. See PagePlus Help for
more information.

Gradient and bitmap fills

Gradient fills provide a gradation or spectrum of colours spreading
between two or more points on an object. A gradient fill has an editable
path with handles that mark the origin of each of these key colours. A
bitmap fill uses a named bitmap—often a material, pattern, or
background image—to fill an object.

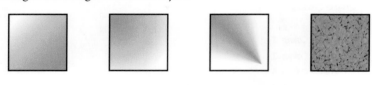

Linear   *Elliptical*   *Conical*   *Bitmap*

You can apply preset gradient and bitmap fills from the Swatches tab to the fill or outline of a shape or **text frame**. **Table cells** as well as **artistic**, **frame**, and table text can also take a gradient or bitmap fill. The fill's path on an object's fill or line can also be varied for different effects (see PagePlus Help).

Applying a gradient or bitmap fill

There are several ways to apply a gradient or bitmap fill: using the **Swatches** tab, the **Fill Tool**, or the **Fill** dialog.

PagePlus can also produce automatic gradient fills based on applied solid colours—giving you an almost unlimited number of choices.

To apply an automatic gradient:

1. Select an object with a **solid colour applied** to its fill, outline, and/or text.

2. From the Colour toolbar's **Fill**, **Line** or **Text** buttons, select an Automatic gradient that blends from the current colour to white or black.

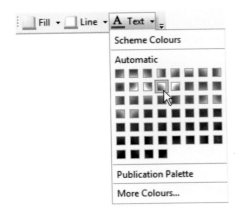

To apply a preset gradient or bitmap fill using the Swatches tab:

1.   Display the Swatches tab and ensure either **Fill**, **Line**, or **Text** is selected (for an object's fill, outline, or text fill respectively). The colour of the underline reflects the colour of your selected object.

2.   For gradient fills, select a gradient category, e.g. Linear, Elliptical, etc., from the **Gradient** button's drop-down list.
      - or -

      For bitmap fills, select a drop-down list category from the **Bitmap** button.

3.   Select the object(s), and then click the appropriate gallery swatch for the fill you want to apply.
      - or -

      Drag a gallery swatch onto any object (it doesn't need to be selected) and release the mouse button. This will affect the object's Fill but not its Line or Text fill.

4.   If needed, adjust the fill's **Tint** at the bottom of the tab with the tab slider or set a percentage value in the input box.

Applying different transparency effects (using the **Transparency** tab) won't alter the object's fill settings as such, but may significantly alter a fill's actual appearance.

To apply a gradient fill with the Fill Tool:

1.   Select an object.

2.   Click the **Fill Tool** on the **Attributes** toolbar.

3.  Display the Swatches tab and ensure **Fill**, **Line**, or **Text** is selected (for an object's fill, outline, or text fill respectively). The colour of the underline reflects the colour of your selected object.

4. Click and drag on the object to define the fill path. The object takes a simple Linear fill, grading from the object's current colour to monochrome white.

If the object is white already (or has no fill), grading is from white to black.

You can modify the gradient further using the context toolbar.

To modify a gradient start and end colours using the context toolbar:

1. With the object selected, click the Fill Tool on the **Attributes** toolbar.

2. On the context toolbar:

    • Choose the fill type from the drop-down list. (You can also apply a **Solid** or **None** fill type.)

- From the **Start Colour** drop-down list, select a colour or click **More Colours** to display the **Colour Selector** dialog.

  You can also apply an **End Colour** in the same way.
  - or -

  For **Three** or **Four Colour** only, select an object's fill handle and select a colour from the **Fill Colour** drop-down list.

Alternatively, a dialog can be used to add or subtract **key colours** from the gradient, apply different key colours to individual handles, or vary the overall shading of the effect applied to the object.

Editing the fill path

When you select a fillable object, the **Fill Tool** becomes available (otherwise it's greyed out). When you select the Fill Tool, if the object uses a **gradient fill**, you'll see the **fill path** displayed as a line, with handles marking where the spectrum between each key colour begins and ends. Adjusting the handle positions determines the actual spread of colours between handles. You can also edit a gradient fill by adding, deleting, or changing key colours.

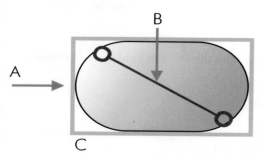

(A) Linear Fill based on key colours, (B) Path, (C) Effect on Object

To adjust the gradient fill path on a selected object:

1. Display the Swatches tab and ensure **Fill**, **Line**, or **Text** is selected (for an object's fill, outline, or text fill respectively).

   Note that the colour of the underline reflects the colour of your selected object.

2. Click the **Fill Tool** on the **Attributes** toolbar. The fill path appears on the object's fill, outline, or text content.

3. Use the **Fill Tool** to drag the start and end path handles, or click on the object for a new start handle and drag out a new fill path. The gradient starts where you place the start handle, and ends where you place the end handle.

Each gradient fill type has a characteristic path. For example, Linear fills have single-line paths, while Radial fills have a two-line path so you can adjust the fill's extent in two directions away from the centre. If the object uses a **bitmap fill**, you'll see the fill path displayed as two lines joined at a centre point. Handles mark the fill's centre and edges.

Working with transparency

Transparency effects are great for highlights, shading and shadows, and simulating "rendered" realism. They can make the critical difference between flat-looking publications and publications with depth and snap. PagePlus fully supports variable transparency and lets you apply solid, gradient, or bitmap transparency to an object's fill or outline easily.

For example, in the illustration below, the butterflies have a solid (100% opaque) transparency, a gradient (100% to 0% opaque) transparency and a solid (50% opaque) transparency from left to right.

Transparencies work rather like fills that use "disappearing ink" instead of colour. The more transparency in a particular spot, the more "disappearing" takes place there, and the more the object(s) underneath show through.

Just as a **gradient fill** can vary from light to dark, a transparency can vary from more to less, i.e. from clear to opaque, as in the illustration:

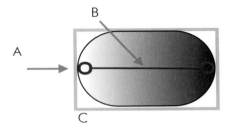

(A) Linear Transparency, (B) Path, (C) Effect on Object

Transparency types available in the Transparency tab are as follows:

- **Solid** transparency distributes the transparency uniformly.

- **Gradient** transparencies include linear, elliptical, and conical effects, ranging from clear to opaque.

- **Bitmap** transparencies include categorized texture maps based on the Swatches tab's selection of bitmaps.

Applying transparency

You can apply transparency to shapes, **text frames**, table cells, and to any **artistic**, **frame**, and table text.

To apply transparency with Transparency tab:

1.   With your object selected, display the Transparency tab and ensure either **Fill** or **Line** is selected (for an object's fill or outline, respectively).

2.   For solid transparency, select the   **Solid** button and pick a thumbnail from the solid transparency gallery. The lighter thumbnails represent more transparency (expressed as percentage).

- or -

For gradient transparency, choose the [ ] **Gradient** button and pick your thumbnail.

- or -

For bitmap transparency, choose the [ ] ▾ **Bitmap** button and pick a thumbnail from a range of categories.

The transparency is applied to the object's fill or outline.

3. Alternatively, drag the desired thumbnail from the gallery to an object, and release the mouse button.

To apply gradient transparency with the Transparency Tool:

1. Select the object and set the Transparency tab's Fill/Line swatch as before.

2. Click the [ ] **Transparency Tool** on the **Attributes** toolbar.

3. Drag your cursor across the object and release the mouse button. The object takes a simple Linear transparency, grading from 100% opacity to 0% opacity (fully transparent).

Editing transparency

Once you've applied a gradient transparency, you can adjust or replace its **path** on the object, and the **level** of transparency along the path. You can even create more complex transparency effects by adding extra handles to the path by clicking and assigning different levels to each handle.

To adjust the transparency path:

- Use the ⛌ **Transparency Tool** to drag individual handles, or click on the object for a new start handle and drag out a new transparency path. The effect starts where you place the start handle, and ends where you place the end handle. For bitmap transparencies, the path determines the centre and two edges of the effect.

Editing a **gradient transparency** path is similar to editing a comparable **fill path**. Adding a level of transparency means varying the transparency gradient by introducing a new **handle** and assigning it a particular value. For transparencies with multiple handles, each handle has its own value, comparable to a key colour in a gradient fill. Note that you cannot alter the values in a bitmap transparency.

To edit a gradient transparency directly:

1. Select the object and set the Transparency tab's **Fill/Line** swatch as before.

2. Click the ⛌ **Transparency Tool** on the **Attributes** toolbar. The object's transparency path appears on the fill or line, with start and end handles.

3. To **add** a transparency handle, drag from any **solid transparency** sample in the Transparency tab to the point on the path where you want to add the handle.

The higher the percentage value assigned to a transparency handle, the more transparent the effect at that point. Note: The hue of the colour doesn't matter, only its percentage value—so it's much easier just to choose from the set of gallery thumbnails.

4.   To **change** the transparency value of any existing handle, including the start and end handles, select the handle and click on a new thumbnail in the Transparency tab's Solid transparency gallery (you can also drag your chosen thumbnail onto the selected handle).

5.   To **move** a handle you've added, simply drag it to a new position along the transparency path.

6.   To **delete** a handle you've added, select it and press the **Delete** key.

Publishing and Sharing

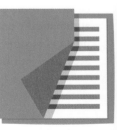

9

Preflight check

Preflight is an essential process to ensure that your PagePlus output, whether PDF, HTML or eBook (both EPUB and EPUB 3 Fixed Layout), is published as intended. You can run a preflight check at any time during your design process to fix issues as they occur. In addition, when a problem is encountered on publishing, the preflight check will report the problem in the **Preflight** tab automatically, allowing you to check, locate, and fix the problem.

The example below shows elements of the page design which may generate warnings if publishing a document as a PDF

(A) Missing font style, (B) Low resolution image, (C) Unsupported form object, (D) Small hyperlink area, (E) Incompatible audio file

It is not mandatory to resolve the warnings indicated in the Preflight check, in some cases PagePlus will work around the problem automatically on publication. However, by resolving the warnings, your final publication should provide users with a better experience when accessing your chosen output.

Manual preflight check

Checking your publication as you design is particularly useful when working toward a specific output which must comply with a rigid layout and style, such as HTML or eBook. You can then resolve problems as they arise, saving you time when you finally come to publish your publication.

To run a manual Preflight check:

1. Click **Preflight** at the bottom of your workspace to view the **Preflight** tab.

2. In the tab's drop-down list, select the desired publication type.

3. Click **Check** to run the preflight check.

    Any warnings will be listed in the **Preflight** tab.

> ⚠ Some warnings may not be displayed during a manual preflight check as some problems are only specific to options chosen in the relevant Publish as dialogs.

To resolve problems listed in the Preflight check:

1. Select a warning from the list. A brief explanation of the warning displays at the bottom of the **Preflight** tab.

2. (Optional) Click **Help** to get immediate help on how to resolve your publishing problem.

3. Click **Locate** to automatically select the problem object.

4. Modify the object as appropriate.

   - or -

   Click **Fix** to resolve the publishing problem automatically (not valid for all warnings).

5. (Optional) Click **Check** to run the preflight check again.

   This is useful once you've resolved a problem and you need to verify your fix before republishing.

Automated preflight check

PagePlus will automatically run a check of your document when you publish. This automated check is more comprehensive than the manual check **discussed above** as it also covers the options set in the Publish as dialogs. If there are any problems with the publication, the **Preflight** tab will automatically open, displaying a list of issues.

A warning dialog will also display, asking whether you wish to proceed with the export and ignore the listed problems. Click **Yes** to continue with publication or **No** to work through the issues before publishing.

To resolve the listed problems, follow the steps listed.

Interactive Print/PDF Preview

The **Print/PDF Preview** mode changes the screen view to display your page layout without frames, guides, rulers, and other screen items. Supporting toolbars allow for a comprehensive and interactive preview of your publication pages before **printing** or **publishing as PDF**.

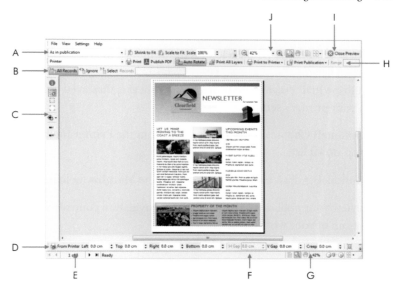

(**A**) Imposition toolbar, (**B**) Mail and Photo Merge toolbar (hidden by default), (**C**) Page Marks toolbar, (**D**) Margins toolbar, (**E**) Page Navigation tools, (**F**) Hintline toolbar, (**G**) View tools, (**H**) Printer toolbar, (**I**) Close toolbar, (**J**) View toolbar (hidden by default).

The Preview is interactive—its main feature is to provide dynamic **print-time** imposition. Put simply, this allows you to create folded books, booklets, and more, **at the printing/publication stage** from unfolded basic publication setups. Other interactive features are also available while in Preview mode.

- Select installed printers, and choose which pages to print and how they print (to printer, file or separation).

- Add and adjust printer **margins**.

- Switch on/off **page marks** when generating professional output.

- Control which database records print when using mail and photo merge via a **Mail and Photo Merge toolbar**.

To preview the page:

1.   Click [icon] **Print/PDF Preview** on the **Standard** toolbar.

     In Print/PDF Preview, your first printer sheet is displayed according to your printer's setup.

2.   (Optional) Choose an installed printer from the **Printer** toolbar's drop-down list.

3.   (Optional) Adjust printer margins from the **Margins** toolbar.

4.   Review your publication using the page navigation controls at the bottom of your workspace.

To print via Printer toolbar:

1.   Choose which page to print via the toolbar's **Print Publication** drop-down list. For 'Print Specific Pages', type page number(s) into the **Range** box.

2.   Select [icon] **Print**.

The standard **Print** dialog is then displayed, where settings are carried over from Preview mode (see **Printing basics** on p. 118).

To publish as PDF via Printer toolbar:

•   Select [icon] **Publish PDF**.

The standard **Publish PDF** dialog is then displayed (see **Publishing PDF files** on p. 120).

To cancel Preview mode:

•   Select [icon] **Close Preview** from the top of your workspace (or click the window's [X] **Close** button).

Document imposition in Preview mode

During preview, you can enable imposition of your document, choosing a mode suited to your intended final publication (book, booklet, etc.). Each mode displays different toolbar options on the context-sensitive **Imposition** toolbar. Document imposition is not limited to desktop printing—it can also be used when creating a press-ready PDF for professional printing.

To choose an imposition mode:

- From the **Imposition** toolbar, select an option from the **Imposition Mode** drop-down list.

Printing books and booklets

To produce double-sided sheets, click **Print** and use the Print dialog's Double-sided Printing or Manual Duplex options (under More Options). Ensure your printer is setup for double-sided printing or run sheets through twice, printing first the front and then the back of the sheet (reverse top and bottom between runs). The sheets can then be collated and bound at their centre to produce a booklet, with all the pages in the correct sequence.

Printing basics

Printing your publication to a desktop printer is one of the more likely operations you'll be performing in PagePlus. The easy-to-use Print dialog presents the most commonly used options to you, with a navigable "live" Preview window to check your print output.

The dialog also supports additional printing options via the **More Options** button including **Double-sided Printing**, **Mail Merge**, **Rasterize**, and many other useful printing options. One particular option, called **Layout**, allows for print-time imposition of your publication—simply create a booklet or other folded publication at the print stage.

Here we'll cover what you need to know for basic desktop printer output. If you're working with a service bureau or professional printer and need to provide PDF output, see **Publishing PDF files** (p. 120).

To set up your printer or begin printing:

1. (Optional) To print selected text or objects, make your selection on the page.

2. Click **Print** on the **Standard** toolbar. The **Print** dialog appears.

To set your printing options:

1. Select a currently installed printer from the **Printer** drop-down list. If necessary, click the **Properties** button to set up the printer for the correct page size, etc.

2. Select a printer profile from the **Profile** drop-down list. You can just use **Current Settings** or choose a previously saved custom profile (.ppr) based on a combination of dialog settings; **Browse** lets you navigate to any .ppr file on your computer. To save current settings, click the **Save As** button, and provide a unique profile name. The profile is added to the drop-down list.

If you modify a profile's setting, an asterisk appears next to its name.

3. Select the number of copies to print, and optionally instruct the printer to **Collate** them.

4. Select the print **Range** to be printed, e.g. the Entire Publication, Current Page, Current Selection (if selected text or objects in step 1), or range of pages. For specific pages or a range of pages, enter "1,3,5" or "2-5", or enter any combination of the two.

   Whichever option you've chosen, the **Include** drop-down list lets you export all sheets in the range, or just odd or even sheets, with the option of printing in **Reverse** order.

5. Set a percentage **Scale** which will enlarge or shrink your print output (both page and contents). A 100% scale factor creates a full size print output. Alternatively, from the adjacent drop-down list, choose **Shrink to Fit** to reduce your publication's page size to the printer sheet size or **Scale to Fit** to enlarge or reduce the publication page size as required.

6. Keep **Auto Rotate** checked if you want your publication page to automatically rotate your printer's currently set sheet orientation. When you access the Print dialog, if page and sheet sizes do not match, you'll be prompted to adjust your printer sheet orientation automatically (or you can just ignore auto-rotation).

7. Select an option from the **Work around printer problems** drop-down list. **Best Quality** is selected by default, but occasionally problems arise with some printer drivers when bitmaps in a publication use transparency. If you are getting poor results, you can select the **Send As Bitmap** option to output whole pages as bitmaps. While slower, this approach virtually guarantees successful printing.

8. Click **Print**.

Trimmed Mode

Trimmed Mode is similar to **Print/PDF Preview**, letting you view your page exactly how it will appear in print. Visible guides, objects partly on the pasteboard, text marks, and special characters will all be hidden so your preview is realistic.

To enter trimmed mode:

- From the **View** menu, click **Trimmed Mode**.

You can select the option again to exit Trimmed Mode.

> Objects are cropped by the page boundaries, not the print boundaries.
>
> You can still edit page content while Trimmed Mode is enabled.

More print options

Additional print options are available from the Print dialog if you're planning to use **imposition at print time** (see p. 117), use specific PagePlus features which use printing (e.g., **Mail Merge**), **print double-sided**, or generate professional output.

Publishing PDF files

PagePlus can output your publications to PDF (Portable Document Format), a cross-platform WYSIWYG file format developed by Adobe, intended to handle documents in a device- and platform-independent manner.

PDF documents are ideal for both **web-ready** distribution and **professional** printing.

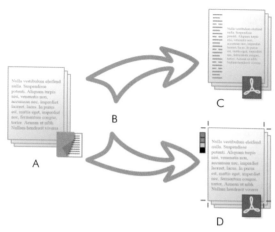

(A) PagePlus Publication, (B) Preflight and Publish, (C) web-ready PDF, (D) Press-ready PDF (professional).

In PagePlus, ready-to-go PDF profiles are available for both uses, making PDF setup less complicated.

Preflight checking

To assist you as you design, you can perform a manual preflight check as you go. On publishing, a preflight check is also run automatically, alerting you to any design problems that would result in sub-optimal published results. See **Preflight check** on p. 112 for more information.

The preflight check also offers solutions to resolve PDF publishing issues.

Publishing to PDF

To publish as a PDF file (using a profile):

1. Click **Publish as PDF** on the **Standard** toolbar.

2. Select a profile for screen-ready or professional output from the **Profile** drop-down list.

   The dialog updates with the selected profile's new settings. The **Compatibility** is set according to the profile and doesn't need to be changed.

3. Select the **Range** to be published, e.g. the Entire Publication, Current Page, or range of pages. For specific pages or a range of pages, enter "1,3,5" or "2-5", or enter any combination of the two .

4. Set a percentage **Scale** which will enlarge or shrink your published output (both page and contents). A 100% scale factor creates a full size print output.

5. (Optional) Click **More Options** and make any additional settings as required.

6. Click **Publish**.

For a detailed explanation of each export setting see PagePlus Help.

Saving PDF profiles

To save any current combination of your own PDF output settings as a custom publish profile with a unique name, click the **Save As** button next to the Profile drop-down list. Type in a new name and click **Save**. In a subsequent session you can recall the profile by selecting its name from the list.

Publishing as eBooks

In PagePlus, you can be your own publisher and create flowing eBooks in both EPUB and Kindle mobi formats, and fixed-layout eBooks in EPUB 3 format. Like **publishing to PDF** and HTML, the process of eBook publishing is straightforward, with the added benefit of manual and automatic **preflight checking** to ensure your file conforms to eBook standards.

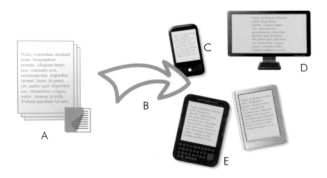

*(**A**) PagePlus Publication, (**B**) Preflight and Publish, (**C**) Smart phone, (**D**) Computer, (**E**) Kindle/EPUB readers.*

Preflight checking

To assist you as you design, you can perform a manual preflight check as you go. On publishing, a preflight check is also run automatically, alerting you to any design problems that would result in sub-optimal published results. See **Preflight check** on p. 112 for more information.

The preflight check also offers solutions to resolve EPUB 2 and EPUB 3 publishing warnings (see PagePlus Help).

Publishing

Different approaches can be taken depending on whether you are
publishing flowing or fixed-layout eBooks, and which file format you
wish to publish, i.e. EPUB or Kindle mobi. All the eBook publishing
processes are similar, except that they create different files (i.e., *.mobi,
*.epub (v2), and *.epub (v3)). Kindle publishing additionally requires
the KindleGen program to be **installed on your computer**.

To publish a flowing or fixed layout eBook:

1. Choose **Publish As**> from the **File** menu and select **eBook**
    from the submenu.

2. With the Output menu item selected, from the **Profile** drop-
    down menu select a flowing or fixed option according to the
    type of device you want to publish to. Alternatively, ignore
    profiles to fully customize settings yourself.

3. From the dialog's Document Info>Metadata menu, add
    metadata and an ID (if needed).

4. With the Document Info>Cover menu item selected, for a **pre-
    designed eBook cover**, either enter a path to a picture in the
    Use File field or click **Use Page** and choose a page from your
    publication. You can create cover art in PagePlus, PhotoPlus or
    DrawPlus).

5. Click **Publish**.

6. In the **Publish eBook** dialog, navigate to the location where you
    wish to publish your eBook, then enter a file name in the **File
    name** box. Keep the **Save as type** drop-down list set to "EPUB
    files (*.epub)" or "Kindle files (*.mobi)" as appropriate.

7. Click **Save**.

To publish an eBook for Kindle:

1. Install the KindleGen program (download from **Amazon Kindle publishing**).

2. Follow the procedure for publishing flowing or fixed-layout eBooks above, choosing a Kindle publishing profile.

3. In the Publish as eBook dialog's Kindle section, click **Browse** to navigate to (and select) the kindlegen.exe file from the installed folder above and click **Publish**.

4. Navigate to a folder, choose a filename for your eBook, and change the **Save as type** drop-down list to "Kindle files (*.mobi)".

5. Click **Save**.

If you checked **Preview eBook file**, in the Output section of the Publish as eBook dialog, the file will open in its associated reader if one is installed.

Once you've published your eBook you'll want to make it available to a physical device as soon as possible. Typical ways that your eBook can be read include:

- **Via computer**: Install standalone software such as **Azardi** or use a Google Chrome plug-in such as Readium to view your EPUB document. Similarly, **Kindle Previewer** software is the choice for Kindle files.

- **Via Kindle**: Transfer your published *.mobi file by copying to your device via your USB port. Alternatively, you can send your file via email directly to your device.

- **Via EPUB device/Smart phone**: Like Kindle devices, you can transfer your *.epub file to your device via USB.

Additional Information

10

Contacting Serif

Help with your Product

On the web	
Com**M**unityPlus	**community.serif.com** Get answers and ask questions in the Serif community!

Additional Serif information

On the web	
Serif website	**www.serif.com**

Main office	
Address	The Software Centre, PO Box 2000 Nottingham, NG11 7GW, UK
Phone	(0115) 914 2000
Phone (Registration)	(0800) 376 1989 +44 800 376 1989 800-794-6876 (US, Canada)
Phone (Sales)	(0800) 376 7070 +44 800 376 7070 800-489-6703 (US, Canada)
Customer Service	0845 345 6770 800-489-6720 (US, Canada)
Fax	(0115) 914 2020

Credits

This User Guide, and the software described in it, is furnished under an end user License Agreement, which is included with the product. The agreement specifies the permitted and prohibited uses.

Trademarks

Serif is a registered trademark of Serif (Europe) Ltd.

PagePlus is a registered trademark of Serif (Europe) Ltd.

All Serif product names are trademarks of Serif (Europe) Ltd.

Microsoft, Windows, and the Windows logo are registered trademarks of Microsoft Corporation. All other trademarks acknowledged.

Windows Vista and the Windows Vista Start button are trademarks or registered trademarks of Microsoft Corporation in the United States and/or other countries.

Kindle, the AmazonKindle logo, and Whispersync are trademarks of Amazon.com, Inc. or its affiliates.

Nook is a trademark of Barnes & Noble, Inc.

Copyrights

Index

11

Notes

Notes

Notes

Notes

Notes